The Dragonfly Effect

Finding Your Inner Strength, Clarity and Wisdom

Samantha Cervino

Manor House

The Dragonfly Effect / Samantha Cervino

Library and Archives Canada
Cataloguing in Publication

Cervino, Samantha, author
    The dragonfly effect : finding your inner strength, clarity
and wisdom / Samantha Cervino.

ISBN 978-1-988058-41-2 (softcover).
ISBN 978-1-988058-42-9 (hardcover)

1. Self-actualization (Psychology). I. Title.

BF637.S4C395 2018   158.1   C2018-906209-6

Printed and bound in Canada / First Edition.
Cover Design-layout / Interior- layout: Michael Davie
Cover image: Avisnana / Shutterstock
144 pages / 35,977 words / All rights reserved.
Published Nov. 21, 2018
Manor House Publishing Inc.
452 Cottingham Crescent, Ancaster, ON, L9G 3V6
www.manor-house.biz   (905) 648-2193

This project has been made possible [in part] by the Government of Canada. « *Ce projet a été rendu possible [en partie] grâce au gouvernement du Canada.*

Funded by the Government of Canada
Financé par le gouvernement du Canada | Canadä

The Dragonfly Effect / Samantha Cervino

For all the beautiful Dragonflies in my life

Acknowledgements:

I have a good family, friends and mentors to be very grateful for. Their love, support and confidence in me are the reasons this book got published and you are reading it now.

As a mentor myself and a parent I want to share my life and my message with you with the pure intention that my life's experience and all I have discovered about myself and the world around me can serve you well. It is an honour to have been given this amazing opportunity to share my life and insights with you.

My son is the best gift that life gave me. I am sharing all I know and all I am as my gift to him. I want to leave a legacy behind for my son. I want to be the best version of myself for him.

I want to empower my son and lead him by example to his personal success, wisdom and well-balanced abundant life. This is also my intention for you.

The Dragonfly Effect / Samantha Cervino

Table of Contents:

Foreword   7

About The Dragonfly and this Book!   9

Me in a Nutshell   21

1: Awaken – My Journey to Self-Love and Self-Acceptance   23

2: Self Development   27

3: The Great Gifts of Energy Healing   35

4: The Universal Laws   45

5: Gratitude and Affirmations   55

6: Manifesting   65

7: Forgiveness   73

8: What About Circumstances?   81

9: Is the Grass Really Greener on the Other Side?   85

10: The Right Attitude- Perspective is Key   89

11: Everyday Is a Gift   97

12: The Dream, Truth or Myth?   103

13: Perception, How Are We Looking at Things?   111

14: Tapping Into Your Vulnerability   121

15: Healthy Relationships Guide   127

Conclusions: 131

A Final Note: 141

About The Author: 143

Praise for *The Dragonfly Effect*

*"**Samantha Cervino** helps you master the power within you to achieve a more satisfying and rewarding life. In The Dragonfly Effect, she draws on the spiritual interpretation of the dragonfly as being symbolic of change from within to achieve self-realization, fostering emotional maturity and the understanding of a deeper meaning of life. She invites you to join her on a journey of self-discovery and self-fulfillment, sharing her own insightful personal trials and triumphs along the way... a must read!"*
- **Michael B. Davie**, author, **Great Advice**

"Samantha Cervino is the most passionate and authentic writer and teacher that I know. In her new book, The Dragonfly Effect she takes you through all the steps necessary for you to live your life by design and not by default. Learn from one of the best and get this book today, you'll be glad you did!"
- **Anders Hansen**, Illusionist, Transformational Speaker

Foreword

This book was written to assist you in achieving your own personal success, a well-balanced life and positive loving relationships.

Follow me on my journey through self-discovery and self-development and all the "roads" that led me to where I am now: living a well-balanced life and feeling happier, healthier and more complete than ever before.

I spent most of my life, up until the age of 39, feeling lost in my own body. That's not a nice feeling to have. I never understood why I felt so lost, misunderstood and at times lonely and unloved. I wanted to be happy and many times I thought I was, and yet I didn't really "feel" happy deep within.

I found myself asking God for answers. I would ask God why was I so unlucky. Why me? But I never lost my faith – that's what kept me going and searching for the true meaning of my life, my purpose in life.

I never gave up because I knew deep inside that at some point in my life, things would have to turn around for me. They just had to. I was not going to settle for anything less than what I knew I deserved: total happiness, love and a bright future.

I will take you with me in my journey to self-love and self-awareness. Through my many experiences and lessons learned, some of them learned the hard way. I have become who I am today: An influencer and mentor to humanity through my work, my message and my vision.

I am no stranger to change… in fact my life has changed dramatically many times over - and in turn I have touched the lives of many because of my fascinating journey.

At age fourteen, I emigrated with my family from my native country Uruguay in South America, leaving behind home, friends, traditions and everything else I knew, for a new life in Toronto, Canada.

Just a few years ago, my life took another dramatic turn, leading me down a path of true purpose and fulfillment. As a global change-maker and Ambassador for The Wellness Universe, as an energy healer, self development coach, writer, and one who has spent many years working at schools with special needs students, I feel that now I am finally living a life of true meaning and total fulfillment!

In addition to being an accomplished leader in my field of understanding and shifting human emotions from negative to positive through Reiki and EFT Tapping, I am also a published author, blogger and motivational influencer through my work on social media.

I've been interviewed by Passionate Talk podcast on two occasions on the topic of Gratitude and The path to finding myself. I've also been interviewed by Mindalia Television and Radio on the topic of Gratitude and Affirmations. You can find this interview on mindalia.com and I also note that it is in Spanish.

So, this book is for you because now I know why my life had been such a roller coaster of disappointments, hurt, emotional abuse and self-sabotage. I am sharing with you all I have learned and how my life changed completely just by adjusting a few things. It was not easy but it was so rewarding in the end.

The Dragonfly Effect / Samantha Cervino

About The Dragonfly and this Book!

The Dragonfly has always been my favourite insect. Although I never knew what symbolic meaning they had, I would see them cross my path and I would always feel so drawn to them but I never gave it much thought.

It was not until I began my practice as an energy healer that I started to be more attuned with nature, my surroundings and my inner self. I started blogging and paying more attention to intuitive thoughts that would guide me to write on certain topics and share them with the world, reaching people who needed to read my message.

One day, as I was having a deep conversation with a dear friend at a patio on a beautiful summer afternoon, a big Dragonfly placed herself on my shoulder for a few minutes and I just smiled. I was so happy and I was not sure why. It felt as though it was talking to me and saying: "All is well, you are doing great!" That's what it felt like as I looked at the Dragonfly and smiled, feeling such gratitude in my heart.

When I got home I started my research on Dragonflies at once and this is what I found out:

The dragonfly, in almost every part of the world symbolizes change and change in the perspective of self-realization; and the kind of change that has its source in mental and emotional maturity and the understanding of the deeper meaning of life. They are a good omen.

The Dragonfly sees what is in a person's heart and soul, they can see and feel past your physical appearance. They bring a message of clarity of mind past the illusion that we may have placed on ourselves by society, family or friends.

The Dragonfly Effect / Samantha Cervino

I learned that if a Dragonfly crosses your path, you are being asked to look through the veil and see the true reality that surrounds you and is within you.

I was going through all these changes in my life, making big decisions and feeling very overwhelmed.

The Dragonfly came to me as a sign that I was meant to go through all these changes in order to grow, create and evolve. I was on the right path and I would overcome all my fears and obstacles in my way.

As scared I was of the unknown at the same time I felt an excitement and feeling of freedom that overwhelmed every cell in my body.

I have never felt so in tune with an insect before – yes, it sounds funny but it's so true! I pay attention to my thoughts and what comes around me during those moments, whether I am out for a walk, sitting outside, if I see a squirrel, a butterfly, a dragonfly at random when it is unusual to see them I take that as a sign. Feathers are symbolic too, if you believe in that, as they're seen as messages from Angels.

We all come across hidden messages form God, Universe, everyday, but if we are not paying attention, we miss it. So take the time to breathe, observe what surrounds you, embrace and love nature.

Listen to the sound of the wind, the birds, the Dragonfly buzzing by. Make time for yourself and just be in the now, because if you don't, you will miss out on miracles.

See the good in you. See the light in your soul, shining through you. See the light that you are.

The Dragonfly Effect / Samantha Cervino

Don't allow the negativity of the outside world to influence you so much that you restrict your growth, success, ideas and actions.

Change is the message of a Dragonfly, change in how you view things, how you work with things, how you carry yourself.

I thank you Dragonfly.

And so this book will pay homage to the serene qualities of the Dragonfly. This book will embrace and explore the Dragonfly values of positive change and self-realization, understanding and searching for the deeper meaning of life.

To me the Dragonfly represents the meaning of a well-balanced life, a life that you are proud of and happy to live everyday. Isn't it everyone's dream to wake up each morning feeling excited and content to face the day, to feel healthy and abundant, to feel love all around and complete? I know this is your wish and I know because this was my wish for a long time.

The qualities of the Dragonfly and what this insect represents hold the truth to all I ever wanted and had been seeking for years. Only I was looking for answers and change in all the wrong places and all the wrong people.

One day I finally realized that the change I was longing for had to be made within me. Ghandi said: "Be the change you want to see in the world."

It was up to me to change my life, my circumstances. No one else could do this for me.

But throughout my whole life, I had depended on others to carry me through.

Despite my lack of confidence, I appeared to be very confident. It was really just a front. When I had the courage to look deep within myself I realized that I had been hiding from the world and living a lie. The only person I was truly hurting was myself.

No wonder I'd failed in my personal life and relationships! How could I have succeeded if I had no idea who I was?

I was afraid to communicate my feelings for fear of being misunderstood. It was difficult for me to do anything that was outside of my comfort zone. And I never did anything alone. I was never alone. I was always dependent on someone else, for fear of being alone.

Growing up in South America, in a lower-middle-class society and household, my life as a child was somewhat limited. Many times I would ask for things and my mom would say "no" because there was not enough money or some other reason. etc. I was so tired of hearing "no" that I stopped asking or even talking much.

I always had food, a neat home and good education but there was not enough for the extra things I wanted as a child. I had not traveled anywhere outside of Montevideo, the capital city of Uruguay where I was born and raised.

Then, we moved to Toronto, Canada when I was fourteen years old.

My world as I knew it was limited. Once we moved to Canada, my parents kept me on a very short leash, so short I felt suffocated at times. Though I understood why: New country, new language, different society. I am not the type to excel under restricted conditions and where I couldn't speak my mind without being judged and misunderstood by my family.

I know my parents did what they could for me in the best way they knew how. But I was a child who always wanted more and more, and I suffered so much every time I was told that I could not have something I wanted, or that I could not go somewhere I wanted to go to!

I know now that a lot of my so-called misfortunes were a result of my own limiting beliefs and pity for myself, though I never saw it this way back then. I was not self-developed nor ready to see my truth back then and so I thought I was just unlucky.

Now I know better. There is no such thing as unlucky. There is no misfortune. There is no being stuck. There is no pity. Here's what there actually is: A whole lot of paradigms that I had to face and eliminate.

A paradigm is a habit that has total control of your thoughts and your actions. It controls your beliefs and your results. It is a habit that is introduced to you since the day you are born. It is the habits and beliefs of others that are part of your close circle, your family, close friends. You grow up believing what they believe and do things in a certain way because that is what you were taught, by others.

In my life there were a lot of complicated and negative paradigms that I, as an adult had to face straight on and fight off until little by little my paradigms diminish.

Paradigms are very hard to eliminate. It can be a difficult continuous battle, but once you recognize what they are and when they are in control of you then you can redirect yourself and win this battle against your negative paradigm patterns, because you – not your paradigm – have total control over your thoughts!

The more I connected with my inner self after my work with energy healing and my studies in self-development and the human mind, the more so many things started to make sense regarding my life up to this point and many things began to change in my life.

But first, I had to make a big decision to change my life. It took courage, discipline and commitment from my part but it has been very rewarding.

The first thing I did was I took a deep look at myself to understand the root of my problem. It was essential for me to get to the bottom of why my life had been such a roller-coaster of unhappy events and why I was literally chronically unhappy.

So, I had to travel back in time in my mind and face my past as well as forgive my past. I had to forgive all those people whom I thought had hurt me and of course I had to do some soul-searching and forgive myself for having felt unhappy and resentful toward life and them. This was a challenge but I did it and it saved me from continuing on that path of self-destruction or self-sabotage.

Forgiveness is a big challenge for many people because it causes you to relive the experience in your mind and be true to it. It means to let go and to release the events and people involved to God. We then need to say: 'I forgive this person and situation and I now let this go.'

We have a bad habit of being ruled by our paradigms, to hold on to sad memories and events and continuously talk about them and bring those experiences into our present. This keeps us in bondage with pain and suffering.

When we forgive and release all that to God, we are truly helping our cause because then we are free and able to move on with a forgiving and loving heart.

It is our lack in faith that keeps us in bondage with pain.

We think that it is up to us to forgive and let go. We think that it has to be on our terms and when we are ready. This is wrong. Who are we not to forgive? It is not up to us to forgive when we are ready.

It is God who forgives and heals our heart. All we have to do is release the pain to God and know that justice will be done on our behalf.

Believe me when I say that I know first-hand how hard this is to do. But through my own personal experiences, I can tell you that this is the best way to live happy.

Have faith that there's a bigger power that makes it all better and has our best interest at heart. The same creator created all of us – one creator for all.

Forgive everyone and forgive yourself. Do not hold grudges and send love to all, especially those you find hard to love. Take this challenge and conquer it. If it takes months or years that's okay, just don't stop trying, because you're helping yourself and learning so much about yourself in the process.

Don't you want to live with love and be in love everyday of your life? Then liberate yourself from feelings that keep you stuck in a bad place. It is your birthright to be happy but you first need to know that you are love. You are the love that you seek and you are a loving being able to forgive and move on.

This is a big change in perception and difficult to do but it is something that will change your life as it did mine. I needed to forgive many things and people and forgive myself for judging myself, for being scared and most of all forgive myself for disconnecting from God.

Once I understood this I was free. Now even though I still have minor experiences with people close to me that can be a little toxic and challenging, I am able to recognize when I am reacting to them or simply responding with awareness. When I react I am giving control over to them. I lose the battle.

I had the wrong attitude and life responded with the same attitude toward me. I was a work in progress and I knew I needed to embark on this new journey to discovering myself, loving and accepting myself without judgment. Oh, Judgment was a big one because I realized that I had been the one judging myself the most for most of my life. My results were a direct reflection of how I felt and believed to be true about me. And I had been feeling this way because of all my negative paradigms and limiting beliefs that perhaps I was meant to live life in a certain way.

The Dragonfly taught me so much and this is why it resonates so much with me even now. Everything the Dragonfly represents are the things I had to face and fight for to succeed. Every time I saw a Dragonfly near me I knew it was there for me, to reassure me that I was doing great and I knew my hard work was going to pay off.

So, the changes began in all areas in my life, home, friends and work. I was making time for me, and prioritizing my time. I realized that to be successful at anything I had to 'feel' successful within me.

A change of environment was crucial, connecting with like-minded people and successful people who would guide me and show me the ropes to achieve what I believe is success.

To me, success is being courageous, confident and feeling complete within yourself, not thinking that you need someone in your life to complete you. Success also means growing in self-development and awareness; being in control of your mind and your life; knowing when an opportunity presents itself to you that you don't say no out of fear of failing because when you fail at something you always have the opportunity to try again and you learn in the process and learning means evolving and growing.

Affirmations really helped me feel successful. The power of autosuggestion is incredible. Here is an affirmation that I still use and it is very powerful when you focus and connect with it: "I attract success and abundance into my life because that is what I am."

I also recommend reading material from Joseph Murphy, such as **The Power of Awareness.**

Writing your short-term and long-term goals on a goal card, and carrying it with you, will remind you of your goals and help you stay focused.

Visualization is a magnificent strategy where you see your dream life in your mind as if you were watching a movie.

There are also guided visualization mediations you can do.

Another thing I recommend you do, is to utilize the Power Life Recording technique I learned from best selling author Peggy McColl: You write out your personal and career dream life and then record yourself on audio.

This is something you can listen to everyday until it will be a part of your being and you will send this right to your subconscious mind, which cannot tell the difference between what is real and what is not. Once you feel it and believe it to be true, then, by the power of the universal laws, that which you dream of will present itself in your physical life.

Make a list of six things to accomplish each day that would get you one step closer to your goals. This is something that I still do – and ever since I started these lists I have been able to stay focused, and my days are so much more productive and positive. I feel successful everyday because I stay focused and I get things done.

Focus your attention on the thing you want during your pre-sleep moments, read your goal cards and affirmations. Set an intention for the next day.

For example, each night before I fall asleep I always say to myself: "Tomorrow is going to be a great day. I will wake up feeling energetic and proactive! I will accomplish everything on my to do list." And I can tell you that all my days are this way, positive, productive and happy.

I will not say that I never encounter an obstacle of some sort or have to deal with challenging people, but I have learned to be calm and re-direct myself when I, by force of habit, react instead of respond to a situation or person in a way that is not favourable to me or the situation or the person involved.

What do I mean by react and respond? When you react you lose control and give power to the person or thing that has made you upset. When you react you are in a state of fight or a state of flight.

Something or someone outside of you is controlling the situation. This is never the way to go as the outcome will not be a positive one for you, or them.

But when you respond, then you stay in control and you think and plan how you are going to proceed in a way that serves you in the highest form. This prevents confrontation and unpleasant experiences.

For most people this is a challenge because the ego always tries to get in the way and want to make things worse.

When you can control yourself and push the ego aside you know you are on the right track and continue in your self-growth connected to your spiritual self.

Even someone who's self-aware can react sometimes. We are human after all and we are going to continue to be faced with certain people and unpleasant situations but once you understand this you are able to correct it and rectify your actions right away. This is being self-aware.

This quality is also something the Dragonfly represents: positiveness, inner growth and change – change in the way we perceive things, experience things and respond to life's challenges that are there for us to grow, evolve and improve ourselves. This helps us to understand who we are as spiritual beings having a life experience in this physical body, which is what we recognize and know to be us. When we die, it is our body that disintegrates but our soul goes on, it never dies.

Our soul is forever alive and you are a soul! We all are souls, and so we are all, in a way, interconnected. We are made of energy and everything is energy. We can connect with nature because of our nature.

Pay attention when you go for walks or are outside in nature, you feel better, more relaxed, more energy, you get a feeling of calm. The fresh air, the animals and insects you see, the chirping of different birds, the sound of the ocean, the different trees, the flowers, etc. and all these natural beauties make us feel better. It is important for you to connect with nature and learn how to breathe.

Have you ever paid any attention to your breathing? Some people get so caught up with 'life' that they forget to breathe in the sense that they fail to take a minute to stop and just breathe, take a deep breath and be in the moment and feel your breath.

That is what I mean. Meditation is a good way to learn how to breathe as well as there are breathing exercises you can do.

Let me remind you that mediation doesn't mean you have to quiet your mind or that you must meditate for more than 10 minutes. Five minutes is good to start and just be in the moment with your thoughts. Just breathe.

To be in a complete quiet in the mind meditation state takes a lot of practice and self-discipline.

When you meditate do not force your mind to stop thinking, simply relax and allow those thoughts to come through. Pay attention to what they are and slowly redirect them and replace them by thinking of a mantra or hum.

Sing it to yourself until those buzzing thoughts go away.

Meditation is a wonderful practice that requires patience.

The Dragonfly Effect / Samantha Cervino

Me in a Nutshell

I grew up in Uruguay, South America. I was a middle child with a unique personality and a big middle child complex. I was very shy and introverted and many times I felt like the main character in the book *The Ugly Duckling*. Until I was in my teen years, that's how I felt. I had little confidence in myself. I had a lot of limiting beliefs.

Both mom and dad worked, so for many years we had a live-in nanny, whom I still remember. Her name was Gyselda and she was very sweet. I have a sister who's six years older than I am and a brother who's four years younger than me. Growing up I was not really close to either of my siblings due to the age difference.

I recall my mom celebrated my sister's and my birthdays together as we are both October babies, but six years apart. She even dressed us the same some times up until I was about eight or nine years old. I believe my sister had finally had enough and one day asked my mom to stop combining our birthday parties. She had her friends and I had mine, and there was no need to dress the same any more – we were *not* twins.

This is a true story! I had hand-me-downs from my sister, we shared a bedroom and I had to share my birthdays too! I was desperate for attention and just wanted my own stuff! Why could not my mom understand that – perhaps because she was an only child? I do not know... I never asked... I just prayed.

I prayed to God for some help! I wanted my own stuff and my own parties.

The Dragonfly Effect / Samantha Cervino

I always knew one day I would have everything I desired. I had no clue how but I knew the day would come when I would have more than what I needed. But until that day came, I was not a happy camper. I day-dreamed a lot, wondered what would it be like to have my own big bedroom, a big closet full of nice clothes and shoes. I guess I wanted all the things almost any girl would want.

At the age of fourteen my parents, little brother and I moved to Toronto, Canada.

It was my dad's desire to live in Canada. He wanted a better future for us and having lived in Australia for six years with my mom and my sister, before I was born, he knew Canada was a good choice. So, I went right into Grade Nine in a Canadian high school and in time adapted to the big changes. Was I excited? Yes! Was it an easy transition? No! But I survived to tell my story.

My first few years in my new country were difficult and challenging. I found myself involved with the wrong crowd more times than not. It was a tough age for me and in a new environment where there was also the language barrier.

By the age of eighteen I had experienced mental and physical abuse by acquaintances and 'boyfriends'. My judgment call was off. I felt lost and alone. I could not find it in myself to tell my parents or friends, except for one friend who swore to keep my secret. I kept all the hurt to myself. I had so many secrets and had gone through one too many experiences that took what was left of my self-respect and dignity away. I am a survivor.

Keep reading as I take you on this amazing journey and I know this will serve you forever more.

1: AWAKEN - My Journey to Self-Love and Self-Acceptance

Thirty-nine years of my life were spent looking for answers. I was exhausted, unhappy, empty, unfulfilled. But why? My life was complete, or so I thought.

The feeling of loneliness and unhappiness occupied a big space in my heart. Being a mother was the only thing that fulfilled me. My son is the greatest gift God gave me.

I made a promise to myself to be the best mother my son could ever have. I make it a priority to ensure he has everything he needs along with my full support.

But I desperately needed to have more of a purpose in life than being a mother and a wife. My soul was yearning for more. I faced many challenges and situations in my life.

Often I felt I was a victim, unlucky, limited in my share of life's abundance, wondering why I did not have what others who seemed happy and wealthy had. I always wanted more and never stopped to appreciate what I already had in my life and most importantly within myself.

But I grew up like that, limited: A middle child with a severe middle child syndrome. Yes, there is such thing as a middle child syndrome, and I had it bad – always feeling like an outsider and misunderstood in my own family!

The Dragonfly Effect / Samantha Cervino

When I was fourteen, my family moved from Uruguay to Canada. I had mixed feelings about the move, as this was a strange and confusing age for me. I left behind my best friend and my first childhood love; he was the only friend that accepted me with all my faults and never judged me. I survived this change and adapted well.

I got married young and my first marriage resulted in a bitter divorce, followed by many meaningless relationships, hurts, and disappointments.

In my head, I was a victim, unlucky, doomed to be forever unhappy. I would look in the mirror and wonder why my life was such a mess asking myself repeatedly what I did to deserve this? I blamed the world and sometimes God for what I thought was my misfortune.

In my mid-twenties I met a man who, three years later would be my second husband.

With him, I fell in love and had my first and only son. I thought I had it all and yet I still did not feel entirely complete. That empty void was still there.

We moved a lot because of my husband's career.

I left my family, friends and work behind to support his career so we could have a better life, more wealth and the opportunity for me to stay home and raise our son. I was finally living the life the way I'd always wanted, or so I *thought*.

My husband's career took him away from home a lot, and for a long time, I was alone and lonely in my marriage, in this life we had built for us. This loneliness resulted in sadness and depression, and my blaming my husband for my unhappiness.

Years later and after three moves from Canada to the USA and from the USA back to Canada and seven years after the birth of our son I asked for a divorce.

I did not know who I was. I did not recognize myself. I was tired of being unhappy and feeling unloved. *Am I not lovable?* I asked. *Am I not enough?*

From childhood, I carried a lot of limiting beliefs. I was convinced I was not meant to be happy. I was at that point in a very low-energy-frequency hence I was attracting people and circumstances of a low vibration into my life.

Without knowing it I was creating my own circumstance letting my situation control my thoughts and feelings.

At the of age of thirty-nine, I promised myself, that my forties would be the best years of my life! Separated from my husband, I embarked on my journey to self-love and self-acceptance. I was desperate to find some answers and committed to my promise to live happily ever after.

I was ready to try anything and I was introduced to Reiki healing. After a session I started to feel more balanced, clear headed, and grounded.

I had a few Reiki sessions afterward and my energy began to shift from negative to positive, from heavy to light and I felt rejuvenated! I fell in love with this practice so much so that I became a Reiki Master. I used Reiki to heal myself, to heal my soul.

I no longer blame the world for my past misfortunes but instead, have great understanding and acceptance for all my past experiences with people and circumstances.

I had to change some things in my life and distance myself from certain people in my life in order to fulfill my life's purpose.

Today, I can say that energy healing brought me back to life. It taught me self-love, self-respect, self-acceptance and courage. I am making my forties the best years of my life!

Just like I promised I would. I feel fantastic, full of love and life. I affirm I am lovable; I am abundant, I am grateful, I am motivated, I am deserving of all the Universe has to offer... and so are YOU!

I am here to tell you that the greatest gift you can give yourself is self-love and self-acceptance. That is success in itself: Loving and accepting yourself without judgment. We are spiritual beings. We are love.

When we love ourselves first, then we can love others.

When we like who we are, we are never lonely.

I had a paradigm shift. I have gratitude in my heart for everything and every person in my life. I love myself, and humanity.

I learned we are all the same, made by the same creator yet unique in our own way. We're here to make this world even more beautiful than it already is.

2 - Self Development

I was growing in self-awareness and was now an energy healer. My need for inner growth continued as God, the Universe, had a bigger plan for me and more to offer me. Although I felt this, I did not know how this would come to be or what exactly God's plan was for me.

In time, I saw the right people come into my life. One day at the school where I used to work with special needs children in Calgary, Alberta, a parent came to me and asked me about Reiki as she'd noticed on my social media feed that I was a Reiki Master.

I had seen this parent before many times but we never really had a conversation before this day. She mentioned she loved my positive energy and I in return said the same about her.

Little did I know back then, this beautiful soul was sent to me by God, and she would introduce me to my missing piece to wholeness in my new journey. When we are ready to receive, the Universe sends us exactly what we need.

This woman and I became good friends and very soon she shared material from Gabby Bernstein, a motivational speaker, life coach and author.

I loved listening to Gabby and learned a lot from her material and audios. I put it all into practice at once.

Soon after this, my friend introduced me to her husband whose mentor was and still is Bob Proctor.

This couple became my mentors and gifted me with books and material that changed my life. I was eager to learn and I was coach-able.

They were persistent that I should meet Mr. Proctor, whose books I was devouring.

A seminar in LA was coming up in a few months after we met, which they would be attending and they made it possible for me to join them.

That Bob Proctor seminar changed my life.

I was thrilled to finally meet Bob in person, this man whose books I had studied and whose audios I had listened to daily, books and audios that resonated so much with me and taught me so much.

I was also introduced to some famous writers, Hollywood producers and actors, and many other interesting individuals that I would not have met if not for this seminar. These people were all there for the same reason as I was. We all shared a common interest to learn more from this wonderful mentor and further our self-growth and awareness.

After this a lot of things started to change in my life.

Opportunities presented themselves to me because I began to LET things come freely into my life.

I was no longer trying to control outcomes the way I had been controlling my whole life for fear of losing and not getting what I thought was best for me.

I understood that controlling really meant me not having faith in God. Here are a few examples of things and people that my faith and letting by act of faith or getting out of my own way, attracted into my life.

I was contacted by the founder of The Wellness Universe and was invited to join this community of world changers. After looking into The Wellness Universe I saw that this would be a great opportunity for me and it was something I could bring so much of my own expertise into.

In less than a year I was a Moderator for one of the groups at the WU (Wellness Universe) Chat room. And a few months after that I was, and I still am, a WU Ambassador.

I was contacted by a WU member, a well-known public speaker and author, who gave me the opportunity to write a chapter as one of 20 authors contributing to a book titled **Success Works** to be published in the near future. I happily accepted this great opportunity to collaborate in this upcoming book.

By this time I had been writing blogs for WU and soon I had a mastermind group with other WU members.

I continued with my studies, attending my mentor's seminars either live or streamed. Keeping my study groups with two different reading partners. I learned how to prioritize my time and make my days very productive.

One thing I do daily is write a list of six things that are my daily goals which are important for me to do to get ahead and achieve my future goals.

My daily goal list helps me keep my focus and not get distracted or sidetracked. This is how I make my days productive.

Also, I recommend staying away from negative talk and gossip or toxic people. As people around me would engage in these conversations, I'd politely remove myself and keep my mind occupied with positive affirmations and a vision of all the things I wish to achieve.

Listening to my intuition together with gratitude and affirmations, I am able to attract more opportunities into my life.

Another opportunity came to me from Manor House Publishing to write this book you are now reading.

This Manor House opportunity came to me when I least expected it, and I was nervous. Although I intended to one day publish with Manor House, at the time they contacted me, this book was just starting to be a work in progress.

This I was sure I had manifested as I had an affirmation for this book to be a success and published by this publishing company. I also trusted that God, the universe, would not be sending anything my way I was not ready to take on.

And so the writing continued with a commitment and a deadline for publication.

I recall the day I signed the contract for this book, I froze and felt very overwhelmed with excitement. Inside I was screaming. I committed to writing every day for about an hour each day. I had to continue to fight off old paradigms, old habits and looked to God for guidance.

I did not allow any negativity and fear of not being good enough to write this book, enter my mind.

Having faith and believing my story was worth telling opened the way for the words to flow in perfect order.

Life had gifted me with many challenges and lessons that I knew were unique to me and would also empower and motivate many other people.

This new life of mine came with a lot of sacrificing and commitments. It was a tough change for me and I had to make the decision to commit to following my inner guidance, and to apply my knowledge in my life in the form of daily action.

This means I must continue to study on a daily basis, making a time commitment, with less social activities.

I'm also reading material by great minds that feed my mind and grow my wisdom.

As well, I'm making a time commitment to mastermind with like-minded people, ask questions and share opinions, gain greater understanding and continue inner growth.

It's a great deal of responsibility to make sure I fully understand what I learn in order to share it, explain it and serve you. Awareness comes with responsibility and responsibility is a choice.

The more I know, the more I am responsible for. This goes for everyone. And I still have much to learn, I will never stop learning and sharing.

I'll never stop feeling so grateful for my whole life, including my past, which I thought was sad and limited.

I look back at my past now as if it were a movie and I realize that all those "negative" experiences I went through made me the woman I am today.

I bless my past for making me strong and confident. I bless all the people whom I thought had hurt me or were unfair to me, because they taught me to forgive.

I bless all that challenge me because they teach me patience and understanding. I bless my present life and circumstance for all the abundance in my life, in health, love for myself and others, shelter and all my necessaries being met.

I bless my future as I trust that God / the Universe will send my way all that is mine by Divine right, which means I ask only for what God desires for me.

Writing and speaking opportunities continue to present themselves to me and I have learned not to say no to anything that will benefit others.

I am often asked to contribute to blogs or write my own and one I would like to share with you now is on Vulnerability as this is something that can give many great insights and help you to tap into your vulnerability. I wrote as follows:

"For me, tapping into my vulnerability gives others permission to do the same. It builds a strong foundation of trust and transparency.

As a healthcare provider, being in alignment with myself allows for more alignment in my life, thus what I am feeling, and experiencing is the same inside as outside. There is a safety that is tangible when one is vulnerable. Further said, my desire is to lead by example.

The bottom line is that we all want to be accepted and appreciated. In doing so, we allow and align to experience the abundance that the universe has to offer, which is already there for us. Being vulnerable is the first step to achieving this."

For a long time as gratitude affirmations had such an impact in my life and because of my focus and belief I have continued to manifest my desires.

My live videos and YouTube videos were of great help to many and so I was contacted by Mindalia TV/radio to do a talk on this topic in Spanish.

As well, as mentioned in previous chapters, I've made two appearances on Passionate Talk Podcast on the topics of self-success (my chapter on Success Works book series) and gratitude. I was also a guest speaker for a Facebook live chat on empowering children.

It is of great importance to understand that you must believe before you see, that faith will attract into your life by the power of the universe/ God, all that which you desire that is yours by divine right.

We are so accustomed to doubt in the unseen that we get in our own way. I call this a self-doomed-fulfilling cycle, where, by lack of awareness and understanding of the universal laws we break the rules and persist on having the same experiences over and over again.

I highly recommend a book that I continue to study daily: **'Working with the Law'** by Raymond Holliwell. Reading this material is not enough, reading alone will not change any results for you but applying what you read into your life by mode of action, will.

"This was my time and I was not going to let anyone or anything stand in the way of my true happiness and career path, especially myself. I realized I had been my worst enemy for most of my life and I was now committed to becoming my best friend."
- **Samantha Cervino**

3: The Great Gifts of Energy Healing

Energy healing helped me heal from past experiences that had controlled my life for many years. This practice was the start of a new life for me. It opened new doors for me and gave me great understanding of my past self.

I felt as though I'd been asleep and had suddenly awakened to a new me and a new way of looking at myself and my life, by healing my soul and discovering my true self. It taught me self-love, self-respect, self-acceptance and to have courage and be brave. It helped me to stand on my own two feet.

When I turned thirty-nine and I looked at my life, all my accomplishments and disappointments, I realized, sadly, that I felt I had experienced more disappointments and unhappiness than accomplishments. I realized I had up until now, lived a life of codependency, self-doubt and fear of being misunderstood and abandoned.

I woke up one morning, looked in the mirror and I asked myself a question I had avoided my whole life. I asked myself: "Is this how I want to continue living for the rest of my life?"

This was the toughest question I had ever asked myself. Tough because I realized at that moment that it was time for me to make a decision to turn things around. I had lived my life with many limiting beliefs, a lot of fear and self-doubt, lack of self-love and a lack of confidence in myself.

I knew deep inside that there is so much more to me than met the eye. There was so much more to me that I needed to discover.

It felt as though my soul and spirit were yelling at me to get out of my own way and start growing and expanding in awareness.

This voice within me kept getting louder and louder and my heart started to ache and in a very overwhelming way I felt freedom of "self" for the very first time.

Though I did not know this at the time, I was starting to disconnect with the "self" that is in bondage with the ego and I was now committed to give way to my "self" in bondage with spirit.

I knew this was the end of cycle and the beginning of a new world for me. I understood I would have to make big decisions and many changes would follow.

As well, I knew I'd be scared but I also understood and believed that I would not be alone on this ride. I felt the spirit in me in a way of happiness and excitement and I felt God and my Archangels with me at that moment in the form of intuition, love and warmth.

I was certain that my new journey would bring many blessings as I was taken care of by God. I trusted like never before and I got out of my own way and gave way to the universe, God to open the way for me to receive and walk through all the doors I had been scared to open in my past.

This was my time and I was not going to let anyone or anything stand in the way of my true happiness and career path, especially myself.

The Dragonfly Effect / Samantha Cervino

I realized I had been my worst enemy for most of my life and I was now committed to becoming my best friend.

It was then that I made a promise to myself that I would make my forties the best years of my life! I knew big changes were coming my way, I was scared and excited but I did not allow fear to get the best of me anymore.

I faced my fears right in the face and that is how I was able to move on and trust in the unseen future God had intended for me. I needed help because I felt lost but I let intuition guide me and it led me first to energy healing.

I needed to heal my soul, my heart and my mind. I needed to understand all the reasons why my life had been such a roller coaster of disappointment. I knew I needed to truly connect to God, to source, to the Divine. That was my first step into my new life.

My soul was a healer and to be that in this lifetime was my purpose. It was at the age of forty that my journey began and it continues on even now into deeper awareness and connectedness to divine source and humanity.

This is the beginning of my wonderful journey into finding my true self. I understood that my whole life had a purpose to lead me to where I am today and I had a story to tell.

All my past experiences made me strong and I could relate to many people and help them with my story and newly acquired wisdom.

Energy healing was the first thing I had to do but I had no idea what that was or how I was going to find the right practice for me.

One day I went to get my mail and met my neighbour, whom I'd seen frequently, yet had never really got to know before this point.

We started chatting and she mentioned her separation with her husband. I thought to myself, is this a coincidence, as I was also separating from my husband? It was not coincidence it was fate. She and I had never spoken like this before. I mentioned how I was going through the same thing, feeling lost and confused and how I was looking for some type of treatment as meditation and yoga were not enough for me.

She then mentioned she is an energy healer, practicing Bio Energy and she suggested I try it. I had no idea what that even was but I accepted the offer as I knew intuition guided me to get my mail at that moment to meet with her and that would be the beginning of my new journey.

At once I made an appointment with her and that same week I had my first Bio Energy session, which changed so much in my life.

Because I did not know what to expect after my first session I went in with an open heart and mind and an intention to be open and reciprocate to its benefits knowing that it would benefit me, even if just a little.

My neighbour-practitioner could feel so many energy blockages in my body specially my back and my chest area.

She explained that the lower back holds old stuff from my past, things I had been holding on to not able to let go of, and my heart was aching because of all that pain I was keeping locked inside.

The Dragonfly Effect / Samantha Cervino

As I listened intently to her words I knew exactly what she was referring to. I understood that it was now the time for me to face my fears and my past. It was time to forgive and release. And so I did.

It was not easy but it was the only way to move forward. I left the session feeling much better about myself and I went back days later for another Bioenergy session with her.

She also offered to do an Angel card reading for me and I accepted with excitement. Angel cards are great if you are looking for guidance and direction, she explained.

The reading was beautiful and the message the Angels had for me was exactly what I needed to hear. It resonated with me and in time I saw that everything about that reading came to be.

One message was that I would go back to school and study something that would change my life. I recall thinking that maybe the Angels were wrong there, because I was so done with school and studies. I told my neighbour this after our session. She replied: "The Angels are never wrong, just wait and see."

And so, about six months later, I found myself studying with passion and I have not stopped since. It had changed my life, my career path.

It started like this: I realized I was being called by God, the Universe, to become a healer and mentor to others.

I started contemplating the idea of studying and becoming an energy healer practitioner but was not sure Bioenergy was the right practice for me.

Intuition told me to keep my options open and sure enough a few weeks later I met a Reiki Master through a friend of mine at a social gathering.

At this point, I did not know what Reiki was. This Master was also a medium and when I met her I was very drawn to her beautiful energy. We talked and I booked my first Reiki session with her.

I could not wait to try Reiki and feel the difference I was sure would make in my life.

The day came and I had my session, the Reiki practitioner explained to me what she was going to do, how Reiki works, etc. She was very detailed and I was very comfortable and excited.

During the session, which lasted an hour, I felt so relaxed and very light. I was laying down in a deep relaxation state. I saw bright green lights and a feeling of calm I had not felt my whole life.

After the session, the Reiki practitioner explained to me what she had felt during the session, she had a Divine message for me.

She said the lights I saw were Archangel Raphael, the healer designated to heal emotional and physical issues; and Archangel Michael, who would assist me with confidence and courage. He was there to guide me and support me through all the changes I was facing in my life. Michael would also help me heal from past experiences.

These two Archangels came to be my rocks and whom I would call upon to be present in my daily life and guide me with their wisdom.

Angels are here to assist us in the name of God. And when we call upon them, they come to our aid.

Needless to say my experience with Reiki was more than I had expected and imagined, so much so that I fell in love with the practice and I began at once my studies and preparation for becoming a Reiki practitioner.

And so my new journey began with Reiki level 1, 2, 3/ Master. I didn't stop having my own sessions though, as I felt better and better each time.

I was feeling lighter, more connected to God and I was gaining an inner awareness as well as more love and understanding for myself and others.

As well, I began to feel love and acceptance for myself.

I was able to find forgiveness in my heart for all those people whom I thought had hurt me and I forgave myself for all my wrong-doings in my life.

What a wonderful experience and positive change Reiki brought to my life and those around me. Because of these positive changes and improvements I was making within my own self and life, I was able to heal and better my relationships with others.

I learned how to really listen and understand people because I had a better understanding of my own self.

All I wanted to do now, was to use Reiki to help people. I was giving away sessions, built my own website and started sharing my new life's journey into energy healing by writing blogs and sharing my own motivational talks on my social media.

About a year later I recalled an earlier experience I'd had with EFT (Emotional Freedom Technique) Tapping.

In that experience, I was able to eliminate my fear of snakes with EFT and so I decided that I would become an EFT certified practitioner and add that on to my energy healing practice. So, I contacted a Metaphysics University and registered for my EFT certification.

I used EFT for everything, physical pain, forgiveness, frustration, energy, tiredness, affirmations, etc. You name it and I would try it with EFT. It works like magic!

EFT is a mixture of positive psychology, neuroscience, which controls your nervous system, and Chinese acupressure.

We tap on the same acupressure points as in acupuncture using our fingertips. It is a brilliant technique! These two energy healing modalities completed my practice.

I was now treating myself and others with Reiki and EFT and all the experiences were positive.

This opened new doors for me and I continue with studies now on the human mind, and self-development.

As I was letting things come to me and allowing God's will with non-resistance, my life continued to change in positive ways. I was then and still am, learning, and not all my experiences are beautiful, though most are.

I still encounter obstacles and challenging people from time to time but I understand that this is all part of the plan for me to really understand life and humanity by having a deeper understanding about my own self.

The Dragonfly Effect / Samantha Cervino

This is how I can work with and help others.

I will never stop learning and growing in awareness.

But one thing I perfected myself in doing is being able to distinguish between ego-based thoughts and actions and spirit guidance and action through me.

When I am having a "story" about anger, disappointment, worry or whatever it may be that I know is ego-based and I know is ego and bondage to ego and old paradigms because it doesn't 'feel' right in my heart, I am able to very quickly acknowledge and re-direct my thought and feeling into constructive action and I do try to rectify whatever it may be that I may have said or done that was not right by my spiritual self.

This simply means that when I react to someone or something and my reaction makes me feel anger or sadness, this is my ego-based old paradigms surfacing again.

I try not to be too hard on myself as I am still human and bound to fall into those traps. The key is to recognize and rectify the action and move on. I send love and forgiveness to those who challenge me, and I affirm that all is well. I now let it go and release it/them to God.

I read that the more we know, the more we are responsible for. How true this is. The more I know, the more conscious I am of the effect my words and actions have on the people I come in contact with. I am responsible to set a good example, to always be kind and understanding, yet be strong and keep charging ahead. I strive to always keep a positive attitude and offer encouragement to those who need it. I expect nothing less of myself and I commit to my passion and life purpose. This brings me joy and blessings.

"Months of intensive study on these universal laws and applying my knowledge and understanding of each one into my personal life I feel guided to share with you what I know and came to understand with the intention that it will serve you always."
- Samantha Cervino

4: The Universal Laws

As mentioned, Raymond Holliwell wrote a magnificent book in which he teaches in detail about the laws of the universe or the laws by God.

I have studied this book for a long time and I never get tired of this material because each time I read this book I see something I did not see before or I understand it better as I become more and more self-aware. This is one of my favourite books, it has taught me well and I will testify that putting this knowledge into action has and continues to bring blessings and abundance into my life.

Allow me to introduce you to these laws by briefly sharing my knowledge and understanding of each one of these laws but before I begin I will tell about the most important law, which is the law of vibration.

Universal laws were created by God, our creator. Once you get to know them, understand them and apply them into your life, you will then start to really live. Knowing these laws is essential to understanding life.

You will learn to release what does not serve you and allow what serves you into your life, by faith and non-resistance, by letting God take charge and by you not controlling the outcomes you think are best for you. This means allowing the universe to send your way what is rightly yours by divine right when you are ready to receive it. It is not 'My Will' be done but 'Thy Will' be done that you must understand.

Months of intensive study on these universal laws and applying my knowledge and understanding of each one into my personal life I feel guided to share with you what I know and came to understand with the intention that it will serve you always.

Most people think that the law of attraction is the first law and I remember when the book and movie **The Secret** came out, people were a bit confused as they thought that by visualizing alone they could instantly manifest.

Let me enlighten you by introducing you now to the very first law, which along with the law of attraction, will manifest for you. This is the law of vibration.

The Law of Vibration - Vibration is the energy we send out. It is what we feel deep inside.

As an example, I know a woman named Mary whom always said she was a positive woman and wished for great happiness and love in her personal life.

But her experiences were not quite as happy as she wanted them to be.

Mary was confused and at times felt as though God was just not listening to her. She said she believed in God and the law of attraction so how was it that she could not attract great happiness into her life?

After getting to know Mary well, I came to learn that Mary grew up in a household with a lot of love from her mother but lacking the love of her real biological father, whom she had never met.

Mary grew up with great sadness and a strong feeling of abandonment that she could not let go of.

So, though Mary has positive thoughts she does not believe deep inside that she is deserving of true happiness and great love.

Mary has limiting beliefs about herself due to the sad experience of growing up never knowing her father nor the truth behind that story.

Though she thought she was deserving and positive, because of her limiting beliefs, she was sending out a low vibration that showed in her physical body by her actions, relation to others and casual negative talks.

What goes on in the inside shows on the outside.

What goes on in the inside is your vibrational energy, which is how you call forth the law of attraction. If your vibration is low then you will continue to attract the same poor experiences as you are feeling deep inside.

Poor vibration equals poor results or negative low vibration equals negative results. The law of vibration is the very first step to manifesting. You know if you are in good vibration by looking at the results you are getting. To get yourself on a good positive vibration I would suggest eliminating any limiting beliefs you have about yourself.

You can start by comprehending that you are not your past and you should not let your past define you. You can do this by gratitude and affirmation, positive autosuggestion, repetition, and a great technique to get you on full force is EFT tapping, which I talked about in a previous chapter.

Limiting beliefs are often due to old negative habits or paradigms which were implanted in you since birth by your environment, parents, other family members, friends, educators, etc.

These can include beliefs that you are not good enough, not smart enough, not pretty enough, undeserving of great love and happiness, lack of confidence, etc.

I mentioned that I grew up in a limited household and once I discovered that I can change my results I had to work very hard to eliminate all my limiting beliefs about myself and my life in general. It is a process and not an easy one, but it can be done.

Paradigms have a very strong control over our life. By studying and taking action you can and will get the results you desire. It takes persistence, understanding and will power.

The fact that you are reading this book tells me that you are ready to change your results and I know that you can if you keep up with the work and commitment to yourself to be the best you can be in this life.

I will now briefly go over each of the Universal laws but I will suggest that you refer to other material or the book I suggested for more detailed information, as there is so much to cover on these laws. I am just briefly introducing them to you as I feel this will serve you as it did me.

- **The Law of Thinking** teaches us that our thoughts are things. What we think about the most creates into form.

Positive thoughts will get you positive results. If your thoughts are constructive, loving and positive this will put you on a very good vibration (law of vibration), which in turn will always bring forth good results into form in your life.

- **The Law of Supply** teaches us that God intended for humanity to not be forever satisfied because God wants us all to enjoy plenty of abundance. The law of humans is increase, progress and growth. Our spirit is always wanting more because we continue to grow and develop ourselves.

We are spiritual beings and spirit is always for growth and expansion. God is our supply and the source of our substance. The problem with some of us is that we believe it is easier to look to men for the source of our substance than it is to look to God, the creator of all.

- **The Law of Attraction** teaches us about two important phases 1- Desire and 2- Expectation. When you desire a thing this feeling sends forth a positive process of attraction, which connects to the "invisible" side of the thing desired. If one looses focus on this particular desire then this line of force disconnects or misses the goal.

Expectation simply means to expect the thing you desire and see yourself in possession of it already, before you can have it in physical form. Expectation is a powerful force of attraction. Never expect something you do not want.

- **The Law of Receiving** teaches us that giving is the first law of all creation and that to receive we must first give, always. Give freely of your thoughts, service, deeds, time, etc.

When we give first with an attitude of offering good in the name of love and compassion, we open the way to gracefully receive universal abundance. When we give with the intention of receiving only, we then allow the 'getting' aspect to dominate our mind and it becomes an exchange.

When we give to people we shall not expect to receive from them unless they do decide to give back, but we should not give to expect the same back from them.

We are to give because we want to and it feels good and let God return to us in whatever way God sees fit.

- **The Law of Increase** "Let everything that hath breath praise the Lord. Praise ye the Lord" (Psalm 150). I refer to gratitude as being the law of increase because when you truly appreciate and thank God, the Lord, for what you currently have and also give thanks for what you desire to have as if already in possession of it, this act of gratitude and belief in what you may yet not see with your physical eyes, this opens doors to blessings from up above.

What some may call blind faith, is to believe in the unseen and to believe is to see. When you praise God, and have gratitude you stimulate your mind by magnetizing the good around you and sending out a grateful loving vibration coming from your being which in turn will send you back the good you want. Praise connects you to God and God is your supply.

It is hard to praise when things in our physical life seem to be sad and dark but please know that to be able to praise in times such these when things appear to be negative and painful, by pushing through in our faith we inevitably force the light and the sun to come through. Every time after a storm passes we see a beautiful sun.

- **The Law of Compensation** tells us that the law helps those whom help themselves. When you do your work the best way you can and when you treat yourself in the best way you know how then you will attract the best things to you.

This Law of Compensation says that you must earn what you receive or you cannot keep it. This law states that whatever we attract we require and whatever we need is always good.

All experience is for our good and we need to see it in that way. There are many lessons you came here to learn and each experience good or bad has a reason and is a lesson for you. There is so much more I could write on this law but this is just a general introduction. For me the study of the Universal Laws has been of great help, and applying them in my life has been a blessing.

- The Law of Non-resistance "True harmony cannot come from disharmony, nor peace from discord. 'Is not this the truth?' I am quoting from the book ***Working with the Law*** by Raymond Holliwell (page 77), and it states: "The law does not require us to work over or against the things we do NOT want but it does require us to work with and for that which we DO want. We dare not give our time and energy to that which is opposed to what we want."

When you concentrate on an outcome to any situation, which is not your desired outcome, you become under the spell of fear and doubt, which only blocks the good you desire and prolongs the waiting for that good, which you are seeking, from coming into your life. To understand this and apply this in your life is a challenge but please know that it is true and if you think back to a time where you resisted something, you'll recall that this thing persisted.

The Law of Non-resistance teaches you how to become more aware and just allow for things to unfold by the grace of the universe and it asks for you to believe, to have faith.

- The Law of Forgiveness tells us that forgiveness allows you to be in total harmony with yourself. You may think of a time when someone you trusted violated your trust or hurt you in some way.

You must have thought that you could not ever forgive this person or situation. But, how did that feeling of not being able to forgive make you feel? This makes you feel sad, angry, frustrated and these are all negative emotions you are carrying within. Your mind is occupied with upsetting thoughts and your heart aches. This is hurting you. To forgive frees you and cuts those chains that feel like anchors holding you down and preventing you from moving on. They keep you in a dark place.

Forgive and release these people and this situation to God and let God take care of them. You need to show love and compassion for yourself and grow in awareness.

This is hard to do but it pays off in the long run as you allow yourself to heal and grow in faith that karma is true and "what you sow you shall reap." There are guided meditations you can do to help you forgive and let go and energy healing is great for that as well.

- **The Law of Sacrifice** teaches us about the desire for discipline and that wisdom is the first desire for discipline.

Discipline and persistence consciously chosen by you will bring you the results you want. This law states that everything has a price and something always has to be sacrificed for something else and this sounds harsh, right?

But wait and keep reading ... We are taught to think that sacrifice means giving up things and that to have lots, you have to sacrifice lots and so this belief may give the word sacrifice a bad name. What this really means is living an orderly balanced life.

As an example if you want a good and peaceful family life but you enjoy "loose" living then you cannot have both because these are two different ways of life. So, in order to have a good family life you do need and will want to 'sacrifice' loose living. Or, if you are a student and want to have wonderful marks then you will have to 'sacrifice' some of your free time for extra studying time.

There is nothing negative about sacrificing things for better things. This is how it ties in with wisdom, discipline and desire to meet your goals.

- The Law of Obedience focuses on obeying: "Obey my voice and I will be your God, and ye shall be my people" - Jeremiah 7:23

To obey means to comply either with others or specific instructions and this can be a challenge to some.

The universal laws are exact and you must obey them and apply them or it will not work for you.

This Law of Obedience asks you to be a good student and a true servant of good so you experience soul growth and have the power to control your conditions in order to enjoy many blessings and true abundance, to obey all the laws given by God, by universe.

For example if you obey the **Law of Order and Harmony** then you will avoid discord.

If you obey the **Law of Thinking and Control**, and focus your thoughts so you only entertain constructive thoughts of peace and poise then you will experience peace and poise as opposed to if you feed your mind with thoughts of worry then life will give you something to worry about.

You decide which laws you obey and you will know which laws those are by looking at your results.

- The Law of Success reminds us we are all created by one creator and we are all perfect and unique in our own way.

Each one of us has unlimited potential and God intended for all of us to live a successful life.

It is our purpose to become great and evolve, to grow and expand our horizons. You were made for progress, you have a life and you either create or disintegrate.

If you look at nature, it is perfect, it knows of no failures. Because nature always plans for success, it follows the law to perfection. If you follow nature's ways you will succeed.

You have so many resources for self-help, self-awareness and so on to help you properly understand and apply all your mental faculties, which you were given by God.

If you use these faculties in the best way you can you will succeed. Success is within you if you aspire to succeed.

Great things are not hard to achieve and great things will always follow those who use the law with understanding and faith.

First you must have a desire for a goal, this will create the power to inspire your mind and if you apply this inspiration correctly and focus on the end result you desire then you will have success.

Start by eliminating the words 'I CAN'T' from you vocabulary and only use 'I CAN'. I do this, and it makes a big difference in my life and goals.

You *can* succeed in life. Life does not have to be a struggle or hard or sad. You can make your life what you want it to be. You have the choice and you have all the tools to make it a beautiful life.

You will win if you think and believe that YOU CAN.

5 - Gratitude and Affirmations

Be grateful and experience gratitude: This is something that I do every single day, since the very first day that a very wise friend of mine explained the great benefits of being grateful every day and told me to do gratitude exercises.

I chose to follow his advice – and it changed my life.

I will share this with you because it works. So, just try it: Every day in the morning be grateful for 10 things in your life. This puts you in the moment with a mindset of happiness and appreciation. You feel both happy and enthusiastic.

By recognizing the good that surrounds you, you also feel content. What a great way to start your day!

Keep a Gratitude Journal and write into it the things that make you feel grateful. Start your days with gratitude affirmations such as: "I am so happy and grateful for my health, my warm bed, my safe house, my job, my family, my positive relationships, etc." (make up your own list).

Then, after your gratitude affirmations, be still and ask for guidance for the day. The first thought that comes to mind is important. You should follow that thought or feeling. That is your gut. You must trust it. This is intuition, God talking to you.

Last but not least – and most challenging – is send love to those who bother you. Try this and please let me know how you felt after doing so. This is something I learned from my mentor and the first few times I did this, it was very hard but it works!

Here's how to do this: Sit or lay down in quiet and think of those people you are not happy with. Then send love to anyone that you are not in a good place with.

This does not mean that you agree with their behaviour but what this does do is to liberate you from that ugly feeling of discomfort and discontent that takes place in your heart when you do see them or think about them.

After practicing this a few times you will notice that the relationship with those specific people starts to shift into a more positive state.

At least from your perspective, the relationship will start to heal, leaving you and your heart clear from ugly resentful thoughts and feelings. When you get to this place you will send that vibe to them whether you are in their presence or not and automatically they will no longer play a negative bothersome part in your life.

Gratitude exercises are my favourite thing to do and they're a beautiful start to my day. This changes lives and transforms everything into greatness. It is a step in the direction of manifestation.

Follow these steps and watch yourself and your whole life transform. Watch your mind: Only accept positive thoughts and reject anything negative that does not serve you. By doing so, start manifesting that which you want!

You will see that gratitude shifts your thoughts from negative to positive. It makes you feel more enthusiastic and that puts you on a high vibration, on a high frequency, which allows you to be in harmony with your desires and what is already yours by Divine right, as you attract what you think about and what is in your same level of vibration.

The Dragonfly Effect / Samantha Cervino

Gratitude is the most important attitude you can acquire and the most life changing. Gratitude helps fight off negative feelings. A negative feeling is any thought that makes you feel sad, envious, jealous, frustrated, doubtful, afraid, or indulge in self-pity etc.

Expressing gratitude is not only good for yourself but also for those people in your life. Because expressing gratitude to others makes them feel appreciated and people love to feel appreciated and in turn they are going to show appreciation for you.

It is the most important habit I have acquired any has made an immense difference in my life.

Having gratitude will help you attract into your life more of what you want and less of what you do not want.

After all, if you don't appreciate the people in your life and what you have at the present moment then how can you expect better and more?

You must love, appreciate and take care of what you have right now and then the universe will give you more of what you want and less of what you don't want because having gratitude in your heart raises your vibration, your emotions and puts you in harmony with what you want.

When you get emotionally involved with your gratitude you stay on a high-frequency, which means you are on a higher vibration.

All of this means that you are allowing your mind to think positive beautiful things – all the things and people that you are grateful for. This keeps your mind and your thoughts positive because you are concentrating and putting your energy on the positive beautiful things in your life. Gratitude connects you to source it connects you to the Divine, to God, the Universe.

Gratitude helps you to let go of anything that does not serve you because you are now on the higher frequency on a higher vibration.

You need to have a good positive attitude, thoughts and feelings coming into your mind and flowing through you. Having positive thoughts, and a positive mind and gratitude in your heart can only bring into your life the good things that you desire! If you think positive and have gratitude you will attract positive outcomes.

I always say positive thoughts equal positive results – and there is really no other way.

Since I started practicing gratitude a few years ago my relationships have changed for the better my whole life has transformed for the better I am happier than I have ever been in my life.

I don't allow negative thoughts to enter my mind and when I have thoughts that do not serve me a redirect this thought and I turn it into a positive thought. Gratitude helps me to do that and gratitude will help you too.

All of this puts you in connection with the source of supply, which is the universe.

Writing things down has symbolism because it causes you to think about what you are writing you have to transform your thinking to transform your life to transform yourself!

Let me also say that it is not enough to just write down your gratitude. Again, it is important that you get emotionally involved with what you are being grateful for.

Put your full energy into it when you write something down. Everyday I say this affirmation for good health: "I am so happy and grateful for my healthy body and mind" and as I write this down a visualize myself and I feel myself healthy, happy and positive.

Did you know that a positive mind is never in the same vibration as a germ? Hence your chances of getting sick are slim to none. And when you write down your gratitude always use this form: "I am so happy and grateful for..." (make up your own list of things and people, etc.).

Start today. You can say I am so happy and grateful for my beautiful warm safe house. I am happy and grateful for my safe vehicle. I am so happy for my job. I am so happy and grateful for my food. I am so happy and grateful for my clothes. I am so happy and grateful for my pet. I am so happy and grateful for my family. I am so happy and grateful for my friends.

Make your own list, as you know what's in your life right now that adds joy and love to your life.

The more you do this and the more your mind becomes more positive, then the more enthusiastic you will feel. You will have more energy to do everything you need to do because you feel happy.

Very soon you will see that everything in your life is going to be better because you feel better about yourself and your circumstances – and your ability to shake your vibrational state and see the light at the end of the tunnel.

You want to be happy and you will start to let things happen and flow freely into your life as you concentrate and put your energy on the things that you have right now that add joy to your life and by so doing you are in the moment and what a beautiful concept that is, to be in the present moment right now. Your energy and level of vibration will increase.

Your level of vibration shows in your attitude and how you carry yourself. What is going on with you on the inside shows on the outside, via your level of vibrational energy. It is so important that you really understand this, because if you are not in a good vibrational state, then you will not be attracting what best serves you in the long run.

Buy a notepad and everyday write down 10 things you are happy and grateful for. Do this everyday and be consistent. You will see in no time that you feel more enthusiastic and begin to attract to you more of the things you want rather than the things you do not want.

Here are some examples for you to get you started on gratitude and affirmations and again, always use this form: "I am so happy and grateful for..." (you can also purchase my book **The Gratitude Affirmations** in which I teach you about gratitude and guide you with some very powerful affirmations that will serve you for life):

"I am so happy and grateful for my healthy body and mind"

"I am so happy and grateful for my supportive family and friends"

"I am so happy and grateful now that God's wealth flows to me in avalanches of abundance, all my needs, desires and wants are always met"

"I am happy and grateful now that I attract only positive relationships into my life"

"I am so happy and grateful now that I am in a loving committed relationship with my desired partner"

These are some examples for you and you noticed I added "now that" because the "now that" brings the future into the present. Whether you are in a positive state of mind or trying to shift from negative to positive, these will help you. The "now that" affirms you are already in possession of what you want. Connect with it emotionally and with the faith that all is already yours.

There is no doubt here that perhaps at this very moment you are not yet in possession of what you want but you need to know that the Universe intends for you, for all of us, to have all we desire as it is meant to express its abundance through us. But we must learn how to bring it into our lives and gratitude, affirmations and faith is the key.

This is how you start to *manifest* things in your life by using this form "I am so happy and grateful now that..." while also visualizing and repeating these affirmations multiple times daily!

By keeping your mind occupied with these affirmations and positive thoughts you give no room for any negativity to enter your mind.

It can be tough to be grateful for things you're not yet seeing with your physical eye but you must see with your mind's eye, through your soul, your higher self, intuitive eye.

As an example, if you say a gratitude affirmation for great health and your physical body is ill, this can be a hard one to do but your body can heal itself if you give it permission to do so.

By keeping your mind positive and no matter what, keeping up with your affirmations and visualizations exercises you will be of great help to your body in helping it heal.

Let the doctor take care of your physical symptoms and you take care of your mind!

Trust, believe and you shall be healed.

All our physical ailments are created by our ill thoughts. I explain more on the next chapter.

To manifest great love the first thing and most important is to love yourself. Feel great for you! Here is an affirmation for that, to get you in a great place with yourself and fall in love with you. "I am so happy and grateful for me, for all my beautiful qualities and loving heart."

Also, try letting go of old pain and emotions that may be holding you back. Write down all the experiences you have had that are still lingering inside you and keeping you from moving forward.

Forgive yourself and others for anything you think you did or they have done to you. Forgiveness is freedom for you and the door to a new beginning with a clean slate.

Here is an affirmation for that: "I am so happy and grateful now that I forgive myself for the part I played in this situation... (you can fill in the blanks here)," and, "I also forgive (name of person you need to forgive) for the part he/she played in this situation"

In my book *The Gratitude Affirmations*, I explain in more detail about the power of forgiveness and I also share powerful affirmations that I use myself. This book will teach you very powerful affirmations for health, abundance, love, career, forgiveness, positive attitude, self-acceptance, money and control issues.

You are a child of God and as such, you shall not experience lack of any kind. Understanding life is true magic and understanding that there are universal laws that when you follow them and put them into action in your life, things will happen for you.

Your perception of things changes as you grow in awareness.

You need to stop worrying as this blocks and prolongs you from receiving what you're asking for.

Faith in the unseen and a strong belief that everything is already yours are key to manifesting and experiencing abundance.

You must affirm and trust in the source of supply, which is God – and it is unlimited. There is more than enough for everyone – we only limit ourselves due to our habits and way of thinking.

"Once you take control of your life and your results and the knowing of how to use all your intellectual factors you have been given by God, that is when the magic happens for you and you start living your dream and are ready to receive what is already yours by Divine right."
- Samantha Cervino

6 – Manifesting

The concept of manifestation was unknown to me for most of my life. It was not until a few years ago when I started my new journey and was introduced to a new set of positive successful people that things began to shift in my personal life and in my professional life.

I started studying self-development material and programs and I became aware that if I know how, I *can* have anything I want in life. So, I will share with you what I have manifested up until now and how I did it.

In just 18 months I had manifested five things that I had no idea how I was going to attain with the time limit I had. I so much desired and needed these things to happen in my life in order to move forward with my plan and reach my goals.

By doing these exercises I am sharing with you in this book, I manifested the buy and sale of two houses, my new desired vehicle, my new job in the new province I was moving to and the publication of my very own first book, **The Gratitude Affirmations**.

And, now we have the release of my newest book, **The Dragonfly Effect** that you're holding in your hands right now. Both books are in addition to my other writings, including book and blog contributions, interviews and connections with other professional that are opening new doors for my success.

By being persistent with my affirmations, visualization exercises, keeping my faith in God, the Universe, and most importantly by not listening to other people and their not-so-positive opinions, this is how and why all I wanted to accomplish came to be and I continue to manifest.

I changed my environment, learned to make productive, good use of my time, and connected with like-minded people who helped me to grow and stay focused.

I will now share with you how I manifested the sale of my beautiful house in Calgary, Alberta when the economy was low and possibly the worst time to sell.

I had made a decision to move to Ontario by the Summer 2017 in July to be specific. My house went on the market in Calgary in March 2017.

My realtor had advised me to market the house at a certain price as the economy was low and he thought this was a great price and assured me the house would sell quickly, as I wanted to buy in Ontario by April 2017 and be moved in by July 2017.

Now, the listing price I had in mind for my Calgary home was $26,000 more than the price the house was listed for so I wrote an affirmation where I stated that my house had sold for the price I wanted and within 24 hrs of being live on the real state listings market. I did this for days while waiting for the house to go live on MLS (Multiple Listing Service).

I visualized getting offers and signing contracts for the sale at the price I wanted, NOT the price that the agent told me to list at. I refused to listen to people talk about how bad the economy was, how I was selling at a very bad time, how I was going to lose money and so on.

I had one job to do and that was to stick to my faith and affirmations! I knew the amount I needed to get for my house and I focused on just that.

The day my house went live on the market I had two offers within the first six hours!

It became a bidding war between two potential buyers and I sold the house within 12 hours of it being on the market – for $25,000.00 above asking price, which is just what I wanted!

Note that my closing date would be four months after purchase agreement for this home and three months for the new house in Ontario. Manifestation 1, check!

In April 2017, I flew to Toronto for one week with the intention of finding the perfect house at the price I could afford to pay. Keep in mind this was a time in Toronto when properties were being listed at a very high price, way above their value and asking price.

I had a goal to look at 10 houses per day, and I did. I was very specific with my realtor as to what I needed and my price limit.

Many people thought it was 'impossible" that I would find the house in less than a week at that price and the size and space I needed and they told me so. People love giving their opinions – but I would not be deterred!

I could have easily just listened to the masses and welcomed doubt into my mind, perhaps forcing me to rent in Ontario but instead I kept my faith, kept with my affirmations and visualized the right house, in the right city with all commodities near by.

I found a house on my second day of searching. This house had it all and had been listed the same week I got in Toronto. I liked the house and I saw it twice before putting in an offer.

When I made the decision I put in an offer $40,000.00 above their asking price and it was denied, but I was optimistic.

My realtor suggested I offer $10,000.00 more. Please note this house was brand new on the market and the owners could have easily said no to me and wait to get a higher offer from other potential buyers and I will tell you that the way the market was going in the GTA (Greater Toronto Area), I am sure they could have attracted higher offers than mine.

But I did as suggested by my realtor and they accepted my offer with a closing date of three months from date of sale (closing dates are normally 60-90 days from date of sale). Manifestation 2, check!

Before the week's end I had bought the house that was just right for my son and I – and, it was in the neighbourhood I was looking for at the price I was willing to pay. I moved to Ontario July 1, 2017 and got the key to my new house on July 6, 2017!

I always wanted an Audi and on July 7th, 2017 I went to pick up my Audi Q3 2018 model. Manifestation 3, check!

I ignored people's opinions and just put my energy into all the things I wanted to attain, affirmations with faith and not a gram of doubt in my mind. Giving thanks to the Universe for having already granted me my wishes that I believe were realized before I saw them in physical form.

I wanted to work for the Catholic School Board at an elementary school near my house with special needs children, because I just love working with these kids at school, guiding them and helping them succeed. I had applied for this job a couple of months prior to moving to Ontario with the intention and goal to start work by November 2017.

The school board called me for an interview on October 31st 2017, and I started working at a school just a five-minute drive from my house by November 17th, 2017. Manifestation 4, check!

In May 2018, I wrote my very first Gratitude affirmations e-book for my social media followers and clients to have access to and be able to download it off of my website.

With the assistance of a good friend, who helped me add details to the pages of my e-book to make it look just beautiful, the book was ready in no time and was a huge success! I fell in love with the book and I wanted it printed in paper format but I had no idea how to do that. I searched for printing companies and found a couple. I sent them the file for the book and they both came back saying I had to edit a few things, the bleeding, the size of the pages, etc. in order for them to print it exactly as it looked on the web.

I am not very technical and had no idea how I was going to edit this book to have printed to perfection. I did an affirmation in which I had said that I would have this e-book published before August 2018 and on amazon.com.

The ebook was published by me in May but I still wanted the paper copy and it needed to look exactly like the ebook.

After going back and fourth with the printing companies I almost gave up and started to accept that maybe this book was meant to be just an e-book only. So I let it go and with much faith left this book idea in the hands of Divine Power.

In July 2018, I met an author through a friend of mine who had worked with a very talented man, whose job was to edit and format books. She gave me his contact information and I got in touch with him right away. I sent him my e-book and told him what I needed help with. He said: "No problem, this is easy for me to do and I will have to done for you in the next couple of days!" I was so excited and I thanked God right away as my dream to have this beautiful book in my hands was no longer a dream but a reality!

By the end of July 2018 I had self published ***The Gratitude Affirmations*** and I had it on amazon.com available for purchase on paper format! The book was beyond beautiful and surpassed anything I had expected! Manifestation 5, check!

Again, I did all of this is by holding the picture in my mind of all the things I wanted with the desired dates of completion. I also did it by not allowing any thoughts that were not in harmony with my desires and goals I had in mind. This was further helped by my not listening to peoples' opinions and by not sharing with people my goals until I had achieved them. I did not at any moment allow any anchors to hold me down or distract me.

I was persistent. I kept with my affirmations and my total faith that as I wished I shall have. I had faith in the unseen, faith in the infinite power within me. I ignored present circumstances. I did not put my energy into what it was right now, but instead focused on the outcome that I wanted! I used my mental faculties to my advantage and it worked. It works every time! It will work for you as well!

A word of advice, start looking at your environment. Who are the people you are spending the most time with? Are they serving you well? Can you trust them? Are they successful? Do they have good habits? Are they an anchor in your life? When you are wanting to succeed and adapt positive habits, you need to start asking yourself these questions and make some changes where needed.

When you experience manifesting and are aware that you made this happen, it is a feeling of pride, excitement and happiness. It is a manifestation that you attracted into your life all because you believed in the unseen, you had faith in your own power within and in the Universe, which only wants what is best for you.

Everything you seek is already seeking you! The famous author Paulo Cohelo once said: "There is one great truth in this planet: whoever you are, or whatever it is that you do, when you really want something, it's because that desire originated in the soul of the universe. The soul of the world is nourished by people's happiness." He couldn't have said this any better.

Once you take control of your life and your results and the knowing of how to use all your intellectual factors you have been given by God, that is when the magic happens for you and you start living your dream and are ready to receive what is already yours by Divine right.

You can manifest anything you wish in your life. Your loving partner is just the same! The key is being specific on what you want in your relationship with your partner. Manifesting the right partner can be accomplished with gratitude and affirmations. You can change your circumstance and manifest the perfect mate and relationship for you. Remember that you attract what you most think about. What is the ruling thought in your mind right now about relationships? If you think that you only attract losers, then you will keep on attracting losers. Make sense? So instead think this: "I attract men that are right for me and in harmony with my desires."

Imagine everything you wish to have in a relationship, make a picture board with the things you want, find photos of happy couples and see yourself as the woman/ man in the photo, look at this image board multiple times a day and before you go to sleep at night close your eyes and live your dream.

With repetition and affirmations you will begin to attract it into your life. To manifest you must believe you are worthy of what you are asking for and you must believe that you are already in possession of it.

You must see it with your mind's eye. If you can see it in your mind, you can hold it in your hand! That is how I did it. Just like that, you can manifest and attract anything you want – house, car, job, money, etc.

Believe in the unseen, be persistent and make room in your life to receive it. For example, if you wish for new furniture in your home, get rid of the old and make space for the new. If you wish for a new partner in your life, make room in your home and in your bed.

The key to success in life and relationships starts with you.

7 - Forgiveness

It can be very difficult to have forgiveness in your heart and to be able to forgive those whom you think have hurt you and to also forgive yourself for the part you might have played in a particular situation.

In many cases we do not play a part but sometimes we do and it is important to forgive ourselves. This has many great benefits. I feel it is so important to talk about forgiveness and what happens to us when we learn how to forgive and let go.

People mostly assume that to forgive someone for doing your wrong means that you accept what they did and you are not hurt by it. And most people never even think of forgiving themselves.

But this subject of forgiveness is so misunderstood yet so healing for you. To forgive those who hurt you in any way has nothing to do with them, and everything to do with you!

Allow me to share this poem with you, from the book **Working With The Law** by Raymond Holliwell, pg. 89, Chapter on The Law of Forgiveness:

"The slight misdeed of yesterday, why should it mar today? The thing he said, the thing you did, have long since passed away; For yesterday was but a trial; today you will succeed, and from mistakes of yesterday will come some noble deed. Forgive yourself for thoughtlessness, do not condemn the past; for it is gone with its mistakes; their

memory can not last; forget the failures and misdeeds, from such experience rise! Why should you let your head bowed, Lift up your heart and eyes!"

That is so powerful! Read it a few times. Savour it because it can change your life. People will hurt you, lie to you, play you, mislead you, cheat you, use you, etc. and you at some point in your life will or have done the same to others. That is life and we are all human. We're here to learn many lessons and we are bound to make mistakes.

The key is to recognize when we do something that is hurtful to ourselves or others and then stop the behaviour. We have a conscience, and to be nice should be common sense but this is not always the case, is it? Being emphatic of others is important. Treat others the way you would like to be treated is key to successful positive relationships at all levels.

When you forgive and not hold a grudge, then a heavy weight or burden is lifted off your shoulders and your heart gets clean. Therefore you are happy. Forgiveness does not excuse a negative behaviour. Forgiveness prevents the negative behaviour from hurting you.

Knowing this now, start applying this within yourself. You will see that to remain upset or hold a grudge, only makes you sad, unhappy and angry and all these negative feelings affect your energetic vibration causing you to experience more situations of the same.

Instead, use your energy on positive things in your life for yourself and others. Stop letting others actions dictate how you feel! Take control of your thoughts and emotions, be the bigger better person and lead by example. Lift up your heart. You have this choice! It only takes the will to do it.

If we don't let go of anger and frustration due to not being able to forgive we put our health in danger. Send love energy to those you find difficult to deal with. Do not wish anyone misfortune because when you do this, you are wishing the same thing for yourself. Forgiveness is freedom from pain and negativity.

Let me explain how our emotions, if we do not express them out and keep them stuck inside, will affect certain parts of our physical body.

In our body we hold many emotions in our solar plexus also known as your stomach and abdomen. All suppressed emotions sit there like cement causing stomach issues at some point in our life.

Emotional pain has its place in the chest area, causing a lot of heartache, a feeling of a lack of love given and received; a feeling of mistrust and loyalty from others. This is how you may feel. Forgiveness clears emotional distress.

A lot of fear and anger from past experiences are trapped between the shoulder blades, and throughout the whole back. This is why many suffer from shoulder and back pain or discomfort (unless otherwise caused by accident-injury).

Forgiveness heals and prevents both physical and emotional distress and ailments.

Lets get familiar now with the term YIN/YANG

The Yang is the whole right side of your body, which is also your masculine side. This side is more assertive and also holds more anger.

The Yin is the whole left side of your body. This side is your feminine side and it is more Intuitive, receptive and passive. This side holds more sadness.

The key here is to have your Yin/Yang equally balanced. There are breathing exercises to help you achieve this and also of course, a good alignment of your energy centres also known as chakras with regular Reiki sessions, Emotional Freedom Techniques and the practice of Yoga are all great for a good energy alignment and clear energetic flow.

Our chakras or energy centres are activated according to what we focus on the most. Many people spend most of their time activating the 1st, 2nd & 3rd charkas, which are the Root, Sacral and Solar Plexus.

Unfortunately, the masses mostly concern themselves with sex, money and material things. We live in a very materialistic society. Since most of humanity is so concerned and focused on these things, they live in an unbalanced life.

Chakras are synced to our nervous system, which controls our breathing, blood circulation and digestion. Blockages in the energy of the chakras can cause us physical ailments. Pain or issues in a particular area of our body is connected to its corresponding chakra.

For example, the digestive organs are connected to the Sacral chakra which is your second chakra. The Sacral is your centre of pleasure and creativity and so forth. FULL activation of the chakra system is very important.

It is very crucial to understand how your body works and the energy that runs through it. All chakras must be kept well balanced and maintained for you to really enjoy your busy bodies and minds to the fullest.

Again, Reiki is a beautiful way to balance your energy centres and get rid off old stuff that may be keeping you stuck.

We can also activate one chakra at a time. For example, I had a client who had a lot of issues with her throat, due to past experiences that left her unable to freely express herself. So, during a Reiki session I would spend more time healing and clearing her throat chakra because this was her most-blocked energy centre.

Reiki is great for healing our chakras, clearing, unblocking and balancing. I have treated clients with chronic pain such as migraines, emotional pain, distress and sleeping disorders. There are reasons why our bodies suffer but we can avoid the pain by taking care of the root of the problem, which is always emotional. Forgiveness is key.

When we go through difficult situations in life such as a relationship break-up, death of a loved one, or the loss of something meaningful to us, we tend to react, in different ways of course trying to deal with the pain.

Some of us vent and confide in a trusted friend or professional. Some of us hold it in, hide it inside, lock it away and throw away the key. Some of us may turn to drinking or other addictions to numb the pain.

Others turn to working out, which is great for releasing the stress, BUT exercise does not heal the root of the problem, the emotion.

Still others turn to their work making work their only and very first priority in life. BUT what we must understand

and learn now is that when we do these things, react in these ways, we are NOT healing the emotion! We are NOT healing the emotions that will sit on our energy centers causing us more pain and illnesses to come.

So, lets see which emotions sit where in our body and some of the side effects you may feel as a result of not healing the emotion or the root of the problem.

Your Throat centre is how you communicate. It's your birthright to speak and be heard. When it's blocked/hurt, you experience a lack of trust and self-expression – and it also most likely will cause Thyroid problems!

Your Heart centre is your birthright to be loved and freely love. You may feel grief, sadness, loss, sorrow, lack of love and many more negative feelings due to old hurtful life experiences that you are not yet aware how to heal from. This causes you immense pain in your heart and you may react by protecting your heart from future pain by closing the door to a new opportunity to experience real love to yourself or from another.

You may convince yourself that you do not need to be in love or be loved by another and that you are content on your own. This becomes your "safety" mechanism.

We hold fears, pain, phobias in our Sacral chakra, When this chakra is full with these types of emotions it gets blocked.

Also, one may feel loss of control or plain fear of losing control in the big "R" (Relationships) regarding abusive circumstances and Imbalance of power in a relationship. All this baggage will cause all kinds of health issues and chronic fatigue as well as liver and spleen issues.

In our Solar Plexus we store old stuff from years ago and even past lives. This is your right to Feel. Emotions that get stuck in this area can cause problems in the gut, digestion etc, Unresolved emotions will set like cement here. So, it is of utmost importance to be aware of this to keep our energy centres and our inner body energy cleared and well balanced.

Forgiveness from the heart and a well-balanced energy flow are vital for a well-balanced life!

There are guided meditations to help you with forgiveness and also gratitude affirmations.

This is one that I use myself and it is in my Gratitude Affirmations book:

"I am so happy and grateful now that I have forgiveness in my heart for myself and others and I let go of any negative feelings attached to this situation"

This gratitude and affirmation for forgiveness will help you to let go of any negative thought and feeling toward yourself and others, and for anything that caused you discomfort and pain.

Visualize yourself forgiving those who you think did you wrong and also forgive yourself for any part you think you may have had in this particular situation.

We all have someone or something we feel needs to be forgiven. To really be able to forgive is freedom for your soul. I carried a lot of pain inside of me for a long time. There were so many people I blamed for my life not turning out the way I wanted it to.

The Dragonfly Effect / Samantha Cervino

I felt victimized and abused for years, only to realize when I finally understood and became self-aware, that no-one was to blame for my life being a mess as I thought it was... except one person and that person was me. I put myself in harmful situations. I chose my company. I made poor decisions – it was me making the wrong choices over and over again because I was unaware.

I was lacking self-love and self-forgiveness.

It is easier to blame others for your misfortune than it is to look at the person staring at you in the mirror and demand answers from yourself. It is not easy to admit that the errors and suffering one often experience are self-doomed. This is self-sabotage what we do to ourselves.

I learned the hard way and it took me a long time but I learned my lessons and now I am writing about it.

Lack of love and respect for myself only attracted people into my life that were unable to love or respect anyone. But that was my company of choice because I did not feel that love for myself. I was emotionally and physically hurt and used, until I suffered so much I could not suffer anymore, until I learned to love, respect and forgive myself. Not until then did my life change.

"To error is human, to forgive is divine."

8 - What about Circumstances?

I've spent many years trying to figure out my life and my place in this world.

And after some intensive studies on self-development, I've learned that we make our own circumstances. Yes we do.

When I met my mentor and began reading many of his books, attending his seminars and studying his material, I was convinced that I had been living my whole life backwards and upside down.

Everything I learned from my mentor resonated with me and made me take a deep look at my life and my results.

I felt in perfect harmony with this new awareness as it made so much sense.

I was suddenly awakened. I had never felt happier in my entire life and things began to change for the better for me.

Understand, that if you are not happy with your current circumstance, you have the power to change it.

No one is to blame for your current circumstances. This can be a tough concept to accept. It was for me. I wished I had known this twenty years ago!

But of course I had to go through all my life experiences in order to come to this point and be ready to accept all this new information and way of life.

Once you understand this, your life will change, as you will make it what you want it to be. I adapted the new habit of gratitude, affirmations and positive autosuggestion.

This instantly changed my life and I started to see myself for whom I truly am, a soul, a spiritual being living in a physical body.

As a spiritual being I am one with God and I believe that God is my supply. Therefore, all my needs are always met.

This new awareness gave me calmness of mind and body and my life began to transform into what I want. I am now manifesting the life I desire. It is a simple concept but it is not an easy one because we must keep our full focus strong and make good use of our time.

By adapting these new habits yourself you will experience the same things I did.

Now that you have adapted the habit of gratitude, self-love and forgiveness in your heart, you are ready to begin your journey toward a new life where everything is possible because you are in a positive vibration and you understand that God is your supply.

You now have control over your thoughts and actions. This means your positive thoughts are aligned with your positive feelings. Hence you begin to attract to you more of that which you truly want, that which is more positive and less negative. You have begun taking total control of your life.

But how do you keep positive when the circumstances are not what you want and not what you have been asking for?

Here's how:

To ask you to ignore your current circumstance would be silly. How can you ignore your present situation? Not possible.

What is wanted from you instead, is to stop focusing on what it is now and shift your focus on the outcome you want!

For example, if your relationship is in trouble, instead of focusing on the troubles you are going through in your relationship, you want to focus on how you wish your relationship to be.

Think of how you want it to feel like, visualize it, put emotion into these thoughts and find ways to bring it into existence with your partner and make it pleasant.

Fill your mind with memories and thoughts of what would make you happy in your relationships and be very consistent and specific on all the things you desire in your relationship and your life in all aspects.

By following the steps that I've just outlined, and by being consistent you will start to attract more of what you want in your life. Do an affirmation for it and ask that the outcome you wish for is a blessing for all parties involved.

Important: You must not put your energy and thoughts into a situation or circumstance that is not serving you.

What you *are* asked to do, is to focus on the things you want instead. Think of abundance, love, health, happiness, and wealth.

As you read in the previous chapter, I shared with you how I manifested by ignoring or not putting my energy into my current circumstances and instead affirming and visualizing the outcome I wanted as if already in possession of it.

You should want to be very specific regarding whatever it is you wish to have and accomplish.

Of course, you may think this is all easier said than done – but with a positive attitude, faith and persistence, anything *is* possible. Instead of thinking something is impossible, think: "I'm possible."

Eliminate all negative words from your vocabulary. Do not say you cannot – only say that you can. Do not use any words that are not in harmony with your desired outcome.

Try a meditation before falling asleep at night. There are apps now with guided meditations that you can download on your phone.

Do not watch the news or read about any negative news before your bedtime as this causes you to fall asleep in a low vibration, which does not serve you.

Your pre-sleep moments should be used for telling your subconscious mind what you want - and for visualizing your new results.

To believe is to see.

9: Is The Grass Really Greener on the Other Side?

We tend to think that the grass is greener on the other side – and the truth is, that many times... It is not.

We sometimes lack that trust and faith in our own life and circumstances and automatically think that we are unhappy, feeling stuck in this life that we think it is our fate and we begin looking for better things and companions, in many cases.

Unfortunately we may cease to look deep into our own environment and give ourselves the time to find out if maybe we are already in possession of all we are seeking and perhaps if we took care of our own environment with a little more love and compassion, then we would see that our grass is greener than anyone else's.

We tend to think that others have it better than we do and that they are "lucky" and we are doomed. This only makes us resent our life and we do not know that this resentment is only bringing us more bad situations and experiences. Hence we continue to feel this way: unlucky and unhappy.

Remember, I said that you become what you think about the most, and so if your thoughts are of self-pity, envy and jealousy toward yourself and-or others then you can only experience situations of that sort because you are in a low vibration. What you are feeling sends out that type of vibration.

I grew up with this belief that my life was limited and the grass was definitely greener on the other side. I always felt my friends had more than I had, that they were born lucky and I was not. It is so sad that I did that to myself. Self-sabotage at its best! And I lived this way for years.

Hence, I continued to fail in my search for total happiness and attracted situations in my life that were all about what I did *not* want deep inside.

I depended for years on people and things to bring me happiness and I was in bondage with that negative and wrong belief. In matters of love, I was losing: I dated the wrong people, which ended in disappointment and self-pity. There was also a lack of material goods I desired, because I believed they were just not meant for me to have. I did not love myself. It took me years and a wise new group of friends and mentors, who taught that in order to be happy, *really happy*, I needed to fall in love with myself, accept myself and forgive myself.

Self-pity is the worst feeling and it's so negative it destroys you.

Finally, after years of wondering and asking God why I was so unlucky, God spoke to me and I finally listened. I thought God had to make things right for me, because I was a good person. I sometimes resented God for limiting my life. I had faith but I was confused.

It took me thirty-nine years to have a true relationship with God, to know what God really is. God came to be my guide through intuition.

I prayed and that was my way of calling God. Intuition was God responding to me, only I didn't know that then, and I didn't trust my intuition. I think I ignored it all my life because I did not understand what intuition was. It is an intellectual faculty we all have and when we learn how to trust it and listen, it is life changing. It is then that you are in direct contact with God.

God is spirit. God is the Universe, the Divine source of supply. God is in all of us.

God is our inner strength when we feel tired. God is our empathy toward humanity. God is patience and understanding. God is love for humanity and love for ourselves. God is in nature and all that surrounds us.

God is that faith we all have deep inside, that knowingness that there is a super power out there. God is all. God is abundance and God created us in perfect form and we are all here to be abundant and enjoy life to the fullest.

The problem with us humans is that we're too much inside our own heads and we let our ego take control of our lives. We should instead let our spirit take control of our life.

We are all spiritual beings experiencing this life in a physical body. Spirit wants to grow and create through us. We were given the gift of intellectual faculties, which I will discuss.

So let go of limiting beliefs and self-pity. Believe that you are here to experience abundance in every area in your life. Here is an affirmation for you: "I am so happy and grateful for my abundant life. I have now all that is mine by Divine right."

Affirm that you have what you are asking for and believe it has been delivered to you by Divine source even before you ask. That is when we believe that we see. You need to see through your inner eye, your soul's eye, your higher self.

Everyone has great opportunities presented to them in their life but rarely do we recognize these opportunities and act on them.

Take a moment to think about this in your life and write down what these opportunities you missed were and think about why you, at the time, didn't recognize or act on them.

My take would be that your ego contributed to self-doubt and limiting beliefs that you were not ready, or educated enough, or confident enough.

Lack of awareness when you may be in the right place at the right time can make you miss out on opportunities.

I am here to tell you through personal experience that God will never bring you an opportunity that you are not ready for.

Our job is to prepare ourselves to receive it, through study, master mind groups, changing habits that no longer serve you, understanding of self and self-growth.

We're our own anchors pulling ourselves down most times.

Aim high and prepare yourself to succeed. Believe in your uniqueness and share your talents with the world.

10: Right ATTITUDE / Perspective is KEY

Everything I've learned and continue to learn through my daily studies for my own self-growth and personal success I learned after realizing I had been living my life all wrong.

I was living from the outside in and downside up. This means I was letting current circumstances control my thinking and vibration I was in.

I was thinking from my intellect, not from my mind's mental faculties in a place of faith, peace and poise.

Sadly I learned all of this after I was in my forties – but better late than never – and actually, it's never too late to turn things around in your life!

One thing I intend to teach you here is that your attitude is of utmost importance. Let me share a quote from Earl Nightingale, a mentor, whose teachings became my daily study. Thanks to my mentors my life changed for the better.

Earl said: "A great attitude does much more than turn on the light in our worlds; it seems to magically connect us to all sorts of serendipitous opportunities that were somehow absent before the change."

Your attitude shows in your mood, feelings and actions. If your attitude is negative then you are going to get negative results and the same type of attitude from others you come in contact with.

By keeping your thoughts positive and your energetic vibration positive, your attitude will also be positive as your attitude is expressed via your mind and your body.

If you have a bad attitude toward life then life will have a bad attitude toward you. It's that simple.

A good attitude will always equal good results and a bad attitude will always equal bad or poor results. This is for every aspect in your life, relationships, career, money, health, education, etc. If you want good results, then have a good attitude.

To develop a good attitude toward life you must first develop a good attitude toward yourself. When you radiate happiness and a great attitude, then you attract the same to you.

I know a lady whose whole life has been a self-fulfilling cycle of doom. She was always feeling as if life had dealt her a bad hand of cards – and that is what she would say.

She said she had faith and believed in God, in the unseen, and she did believe but her way of praying to God was all-wrong.

She did not know that it was her attitude toward herself and life that kept bringing to her those poor experiences she did not want.

Instead of focusing her energy on the outcome she wanted and changing her environment, she would focus all her energy on present circumstances, which did not serve her, and she continued to live a life of the same bad experiences day in and day out.

She was always blaming others and life in general for her problems and circumstances; always feeling unloved and unworthy; always giving to others in order to feel liked, loved and accepted – but also expecting something in return from them.

She lacked self-love and was in desperate need for love from others. The vibration of "need" only brings you more things to "need."

As I got to know more about her, I came to learn that she had grown up with abandonment issues. Therefore, her behaviour and attitude reflected her insecurities and pain from her young life, and even her past lives.

One day she came to me and complained that she gave her money and her time to a friend in need and this friend was not responding and giving back to her as she had expected. She had judgmental and resentful feelings toward her friend.

Deep inside I knew she felt upset with herself because she kept doing the same things over and over again for the wrong reasons. She gave to receive not to serve. Giving with the intention of receiving back from others is exchange. You must give freely as a way of helping and serving others in need.

I told her: "When you give to others, give freely with no expectation of receiving back anything in return from them. If you are expecting that they will pay you back the same way, you will most likely be disappointed. The universe will pay you back. Freely giving is not trading. There's a difference."

She listened and said she understood but at her "old" age it might take her longer to put all this new information into practice.

Unfortunately, she always judged others, always analyzed things and people to find fault in them, so she would have a reason to blame her choices and results on other people.

She also judged herself, resulting in a lot suffering and self-doubt.

Years of her life full of resentment, regret and fear resulted in her body becoming ill with liver problems, skin issues, vision problems and more.

It is hard for us humans to understand this: that we bring in our own problems, and body ailments due to repressed feelings and emotions. Because I studied Metaphysics and how our energetic energy affects our physical body, our organs, I can write this, but I also understand that reading my words in this book may not sit well with everyone. My intention is for you to try and understand and begin at once to take care of yourself. Love yourself and accept yourself.

Have a good attitude toward yourself, love and accept yourself and expect only the best for you, always! Do this and life will bring you positive experiences and personal success. It starts with you. No one else can change things for you.

You may ask yourself now why a person would persist with poor attitude expecting the worst more times than not?

The answer is that we are so familiar with ourselves and our habits from a young age that we tend to take ourselves for granted. We often think that others can accomplish things we cannot. We may tell ourselves that we are not smart enough, pretty enough, confident enough, that we do not have the right education. The list can go on and on – sad but true for many people, for most people.

We do not fully understand whom we really are spiritual beings with tremendous ability to achieve in life all that we desire.

We have been gifted with a great mind and intellectual faculties or mental abilities that when we learn how to properly use them we can make pretty big changes in our life. Your mental faculties are your imagination, your will, your intuition, reason, perception and your memory.

Remember that your attitude is a reflection of yourself. What's going on inside you often shows on the outside.

Think of what you want and look at your results.

Think of what you would like to achieve, of what you would like to have and know that with a positive good attitude you will attract positiveness into your life.

Here is a good affirmation that I would like for you to adapt and read aloud many times over with emotion: "I am so happy and grateful now that I love myself, I accept myself and my positive attitude shines through."

When you want something, take the attitude that there are a lot more reasons why you *can* have it than why you cannot.

The world you have created around yourself is a mirror of your attitudes. If you don't like your environment, if you don't like your circumstances, you can change them by changing your attitude.

Do the affirmation that I shared with you and become the person you wish to be. Act as though you already *are* the person you wish to be.

Time is of great essence and not to be wasted, so the faster you understand this and adapt these new habits into your life, the better your life will be and the quicker you will experience life the way you want it.

One thing that made me change my attitude and paradigm is that I learned through intense study that I am worth a lot more than I gave myself credit for. This simply means to believe in yourself and have faith in God, that he has your back and wants you to have it all. Be happy and healthy.

Always ask the Universe to ensure that what you desire comes to you by Divine right, which means to put in your order to God, the Universe, but let the Universe send you what is rightfully yours by Divine right.

Sometimes we may ask for a specific something or someone to come into our life but that may not be the perfect thing or someone for us.

As an example, I had once met a man whom I immediately felt very attracted to. To me this man was everything I thought I wanted and so in my mind I saw me being with him and I even had an affirmation for our "relationship" but I added "only if this man is already mine by Divine right."

This means that yes, this man is ideal for me but the Universe knows best and I had faith that the Universe/God would bring him into my life only if he was already mine by Divine right, which means "if we are meant to be" and if not then I would get a partner that would be equal or better.

The Dragonfly Effect / Samantha Cervino

My results improved as a result of me just becoming more self-aware and letting things flow freely into my life without my trying to control outcomes.

Being in the moment was a new concept I had to adapt to and have complete faith in. Breaking old habits of living in the past and planning for a future helped me realize I had missed the "now" in many occasions.

So one day I asked myself: Who's in control of me right now? Is it my past self, my present self or my future self?

With all this new awareness I knew that my past self would keep me stuck and not able to move on from my past so I said no, I do not want my "past self" to be in control.

Living in the past does not serve me or you or anyone.

I chose my present self and future self and gave them full control over my entire life and I have never been happier.

If your present self is in control, then you live in the now, in the present. You embrace this moment and pay attention to what is happening now. The present moment is all you really have.

As John Lennon once said: "Life is what happens to us when we're making other plans." You don't want your life to pass you by and miss the little things that matter the most. The Now is all you can be certain of. The past is gone and the future is not ours yet.

The future self is uncertain and keeps you planning for all the unknowns. Having a goal for a better future is great but let's not overwhelm ourselves contemplating the future and miss living now. This will cause anxiety and stress.

You want your future self to have some control of your present by setting some short-term goals for yourself. Write these down and carry them with you on a card that you can put in your pocket.

Look at your goals many times daily to keep you focused.

Make a plan for yourself to reach your goals! This will keep you going and keep your mind positive as creative ideas will flow in and through you from the Universe, God. It takes a goal to make a plan to achieve your desires. Discipline, commitment and self-love will get you there.

Your time is very important. Do not waste an hour of your day on things that do not serve you and help you grow. A wasted hour a day equals 365 wasted hours a year that you will not get back.

Enjoy every minute of your day. As Earl Nightingale pointed out in his breakthrough book, **Lead The Field**: "A human life is really nothing more than a collection of minutes, hours, and days. These are the building materials. And it's left strictly up to us to determine the kind and size of structure we build."

11: Every Day is a Gift

Every Day is a Gift! You've heard this before. I know you have. Have you stopped to think what this really means?

These are not just empty words. There is a message here for all of us, for all humanity. My intention with this book is that you not only read it, but will really pay attention to the words and think about your actions towards these words. One of my favourite songs says: "Every new day is a gift, not a given right!"

When you wake up in the morning embrace the fact that you are one of the lucky ones that gets to see a new day with new opportunities to correct and improve upon your yesterday.

So, every morning feel gratitude and get out of bed feeling excited to be alive! Breathe.

We live in a beautiful planet called Earth, which we must love and keep safe. We are here to love not destroy. It starts by loving ourselves!

Ask yourself this: when you wake up in the morning are you grateful for the new day? Are you ready to confront what the day brings to you, or do you dread getting up in the morning?

On getting out of bed, do you feel your life has no purpose. Are you not motivated? You probably fall into either one of two categories:

1- Grateful and motivated or

2- Miserable, sad, unmotivated.

If you are in category 2 then I want to help you move from category 2 into category 1. We all want to be grateful and motivated!

So, look around and find nice things like nature, that's pretty easy as nature is all around us. If you can see the sunshine, be grateful for that. If you can hear the birds sing or the noise of traffic, be grateful for that.

If you can feel when you touch, be grateful for that. If you can smell the aroma of rain or flowers, be grateful for that.

Be grateful that all your senses work! Because there are many people that are not as lucky. Yet, they are grateful for what they do have and these people accomplish great things because of it. Key point: *"Be Grateful for what you have!"*

When you say thank you for all the things you are blessed with, you send out a positive vibration and as I've explained in previous chapters, this only comes back to you in more positive ways.

Positive thoughts = Positive results. You've heard this before, many times. Guess what? It is true. I am living proof. BUT don't just say it for the sake of saying it, YOU MUST MEAN IT, Feel it and believe it.

Sometimes life throws us stones and when it rains it pours, but in times like those find your inner strength, push through and have a little faith, because after the rain there's always a beautiful rainbow.

Our hard times will always make us stronger and the people that come into our life will most of the time teach us a lesson, remind us of something and make us stronger too.

Even when you feel that people use you and hurt your feelings, and although this is not right, do not condemn them but send them love and forgive them.

Let God take care of them and trust me, God will. You need to know that you are here in this life on your own unique path and that everyone in humanity is on their own unique path.

Trust that the Universe/ God always takes care of you.

Practice how to talk to God and pay attention when God is talking to you. Trust your intuition and your heart. Through your mind's eye, see a rainbow each morning that is your own. Smile and just be.

What I mean when I say: "see a rainbow" each morning that is your own, is that everything passes and as you know after the thunder there is always a rainbow and the sun always shines.

Ask for guidance from above, listen and trust that God is with you always. Let fear and doubt go as these only try to hold you back. Here is an insight for overcoming fear that I wrote in a blog for the Wellness Universe:

The Dragonfly Effect / Samantha Cervino

Fear is caused by the unknown or ignorance, which causes doubt and worry. It can be a negative thing because it stops you from going after your dreams. But at the same time, fear can be a good thing because it will cause you to think before you jump into a course of action.

For me, one way to overcome fear is to first recognize it by being present in the experience of fear and then release it by walking right through it.

It takes courage you may think, but once you understand that fear is an emotion that will pass as soon as you face it and stop giving it control over your thoughts, feelings, and actions, it goes away.

What really helps me overcome my fears is understanding the definition of fear and its symptoms. This understanding allows me to recognize it but not give it power over my life.

As a spiritual person, I understand that when I experience fear I am disconnecting from spirit.

Faith causes peace of mind and peace within eliminates fear altogether.

Remember that you are here on this earth to learn and grow.

You are a spiritual being first and foremost living in a physical body.

The spirit within you is always for growth and expansion and you either create or disintegrate.

You will not stay the same this is not possible you will continue to grow and want to expend your horizons. This is life.

My mentor once said: "The only thing that separates us from an animal is our mind. our intellectual faculties."

We as humans are gifted with six incredible mental faculties. Again these are:

1- Intuition, which is God / spirit talking to us.

2- Imagination, which allows you to dream, create and visualize your ideal life.

3- Perception, which is your ability to become aware of something.

4- Reason, which makes you think, understand, and form judgments.

5- Memory, which stores and remembers information.

6- Will, your will power, which is push and force and usually lacks permanency and you also have your authentic will which is the ability you have to give yourself a command and to follow that command with confidence and power.

You see, animals act by instinct and we have all these amazing mental faculties that God gave us.

If you know them well and learn how to use them properly you make your life what you want it to be and nothing less.

"I've learned that loving ourselves first is key to being able to love another fully. To be in love with life and everything in it, makes our relationships much better and healthier."
- **Samantha Cervino**

The Dragonfly Effect / Samantha Cervino

12 - The Dream - Truth or Myth?

In our search for true love we may go through life stumbling through unsuccessful relationships.

We may put ourselves in situations that leave us not only broken-hearted but also filled with self-doubt and fear that maybe we are not worthy of this ideal life and relationship we desire.

From a young age we believe in everlasting love at first sight as depicted in fairytales and movies.

We grow up with the idea that our life will turn out just like the characters' lives in fairytales. We're all Cinderella and all men are Prince Charming.

As little girls we dream of our wedding day, wearing that beautiful white wedding gown, with our prince waiting for us at the altar – and sometimes we even imagine our prince on a beautiful white horse.

Little boys may also dream of marrying their princess, who is beautiful and perfect. With each new relationship since we are kids we wonder: "Is he / she the one?" It's almost like an obsession.

We grow up and turn into teenagers and experience our first crush and its so intense we feel it as true love. Everything is perfect and we truly believe this is it and we have found our prince who is going to marry us one day. He is the one!

The Dragonfly Effect / Samantha Cervino

But soon after that, we get our heart broken for the first time and we suffer. We cry for days, listen to romantic love songs and we feel we will never get over it as our little heart aches. What a feeling that is – and we begin to believe that love hurts.

In time we meet a new prince and again think maybe he's the one only to find out later that he's not. It seems we follow a pattern in our attempt to finding true and perfect love.

From a young age we look for love with all these expectations that it should be just like the fairytales we are told about since childhood.

Sometimes we get so desperate in our attempt to finding "the one" that we settle for the first partner that makes a promise to us to love us unconditionally. We end up falling in love with the idea of "love."

We enter our twenties and have gone through a couple of broken-hearted experiences and start to think about careers and marriage. We are told by society we should have our babies before our thirties and the clock starts ticking.

We may rush into finding and locking-in our husband-to-be. We want him to be perfect with a great job and good genes for our baby. We picture a beautiful life to live happily ever after. Sound familiar?

How stressful is all this? To plan a wedding takes months – not to mention, money. Then there are the guest lists and the honeymoon.

Most important for us women, is the dress. Oh we love looking for that perfect wedding gown, trying the dress on, looking and feeling perfect. We are now living the fairy tale and living our dream. Finally!

We get so caught up in the wedding we almost forget about our prince and how he might be feeling with all this stress not only about the planning of it all but the finances as well!

As we all know, a wedding can be pretty expensive and before we even say "I Do," anxiety and stress start to build up. Without realizing it, this is how we start our married life, with stress about money.

Our husband-to-be may not tell us about his stress about all this planning and spending, only because he loves us and does not want to hurt our feelings. So, he stays quiet and does as he is told. Does this sound fair to him?

Is this fair to us? We are now entering into a marriage and relationship where there is no open trust in communication because we are afraid of being misunderstood. And whether we are able to acknowledge this or not this affects our marriage from that instant on.

I feel this needs to be discussed and the pressure taken off.

Marriage is a huge change and needs an adaptation period that needs its time, almost like pregnancy, nine months of relaxation, peace and good health.

Ideally, a new marriage is the birth of a new thing and like all births you need to tend to it accordingly.

I am NOT saying do not have your dream wedding, please do! But don't let the stress of it all take over your life with your new husband/wife-to-be.

Do not forget the real reason why you are getting married in the first place.

Be patient with one another. You are going from being on your own to sharing a home with someone. That's a big change and it's very exciting.

Not all relationships are the same. Not all men are the same and there are the ones who will speak their mind about the wedding, the money being spent, the guest lists and other details.

But when this happens, how does the bride-to-be react?

Well, she might feel sad because now she is told she can not have the dream wedding like Cinderella did. Or, perhaps she takes his opinion wrongly and feels misunderstood and maybe even unloved?

Let me remind us all that Cinderella is a fairytale and I myself bought into that as well. Of course I did. I will share my story in the pages that follow and it is because of my experiences that I am able to write this book.

We've now married a man, who gave us the dream ring, wedding and honeymoon. Or, we married a man, who brought us down to earth and unconsciously we might feel a bit of resentment toward him because he did just that.

I personally have experienced the down-to-earth type.

Either way we enter into the newlywed phase in your life with some stresses we may not be acknowledging but it is sure to play a huge part in how our married life develops or progresses.

It is important to understand that stress can be fatal and a stressed-out partner who feels they cannot communicate with his/her mate will shy away and disconnect in the marriage, sometimes resulting in a potential affair, separation or divorce.

Always be open and honest with your partner, no matter what.

Keep the communication channels open and make the time to really listen to one another and never disconnect.

The first year of marriage is supposed to be great, stress-free, a time to connect as a couple on a deeper level and continue to plan a future with a happy ending. Is this not the reason why we marry? But is this always the case? Not always – and the divorce rate keeps on going up! Fact.

Flash forward and we are now trying to get pregnant right after the honeymoon because we are now approaching our thirties and society tells us that after marriage the next thing we "have to" do is have babies.

So, now we are not only paying off the wedding expenses but we are adding on the stress of getting pregnant and becoming parents.

If we are lucky we get pregnant right away, or, as in many cases, we join the women who start treatments that are expensive and very stressful.

All of this takes away from enjoying our life a newlyweds and the adjustment period that takes when you share a house with someone else.

Months later the baby arrives and we realize that is not as fun as we thought it was and that having a baby is a life-long commitment and we come second because our baby is our number one priority.

The baby is a very important and beautiful addition to our new family. We are now three in the house, or four or five depending on how many babies we have.

As a result of starting a family (sometimes before we are ready), which is a healthy wonderful thing we do in life, we sometimes tend to put ourselves and our partner in second or third place and with that may come that disconnect that later results in a sad, lonely marriage.

Many people ignore the signs and believe that "that's life" and this is how it goes after babies and years of marriage.

By ignoring the facts and being misled by society and heredities we are influenced by, we continue on as parents only, and forget about taking care of our selves and our partner.

We may forget to "water our grass," to nourish our relationship.

Resentment grows as women become just moms – nothing else – and men become workaholics (not all, but many do), all in an attempt to ignore the issues, as it is easier than facing them. Key word: "easier" equals "conformity." This is why many marriages end in divorce.

The Dragonfly Effect / Samantha Cervino

Lack of communication leads to self-doubt inflicted by fear of not being heard-understood by our partner; and lack of what we want while not being sure of what it is we want anymore as we already feel we've fulfilled our life purpose of finding a partner to marry and becoming parents.

What comes next? This is a huge question many avoid asking themselves. I am writing from personal experience and if I have lived it then I know many others have as well or are at this time going through similar situations.

Try this affirmation for healthy relationships:
"I am so very happy and grateful for my happy, loving committed relationship that adds joy and love to my life"

Even if you are happy in your loving relationship, still say this affirmation because it is your wish to continue enjoying this beautiful life with your partner.

To be in love is the most beautiful feeling. To be with someone you can trust and is loyal to you, someone you can't wait to see and talk to again, is truly what we all want.

Sharing our love with a special someone is basic need for us. To share intimacy is important to us. It's part of life. So the fairytale is not real but the idea of true lasting love is.

I've learned that loving ourselves first is key to being able to love another fully.

To be in love with life and everything in it, makes our relationships much better and healthier.

Don't fall in love with the idea of love and don't believe that love hurts because that is a lie.

How can love hurt when we are love and love is the most beautiful feeling?

The Dragonfly Effect / Samantha Cervino

"I've learned we attract what we think about the most and we also attract our partners either consciously or unconsciously. For a long time I thought my loving partners had come into my life by mere chance. I was unaware. I was wrong. If I had known then what I know now I would have avoided so much heartache for myself."
- **Samantha Cervino**

13 - Perception: How are we looking at things?

Two people can look at the same thing and each see it very differently. This is perception: How you see things in your unique way based on your paradigms and beliefs.

In the previous chapter I mostly discussed how women feel and looked at their dream of a perfect partner and fairytale life. Now lets look at how a man may perceive this dream and explore how he might feel with all these expectations about his new role as partner, father and provider.

Once a man becomes a new husband and a dad, his responsibilities have doubled. Add a mortgage to that, school fund savings, car payments, food and clothing for the family, etc. and I am getting a headache just trying to put myself in their shoes!

Many women grow up with the assumption that our man will take care of it all. I know times have changed and we as women are very independent and capable, but believe me when I say that even today I see a lot of this happening. For many women, not all, our life purpose is to become a wife and have a baby before thirty.

Most women have a great education and career, but still, many women feel pretty confident that her husband will take care of them financially so she may put her diploma away and stay at home with baby until baby is old enough to start elementary school. Do not get me wrong, because that is indeed a perfect plan and I myself had the opportunity to stay home with my son until he started kindergarten. So, I was that woman.

The Dragonfly Effect / Samantha Cervino

I eventually got a job at my son's school until he graduated Grade Six. I was lucky in that sense, but my marriage suffered tremendously at the same time, ending in a divorce nine years later, not because I stayed at home, but because the life of housewife and the life of a professional person working to support his family, are very different.

I was just a mom for years. I lost myself in motherhood and housework. I loved being a mom but I did not know how to manage my time to make time to connect with my partner as a couple and neither did my husband. This is something that happens way too often when we become parents.

We moved a lot due to my ex-husband's career and I had to start a new life in a new country and-or a new city quite a few times. That put a lot of stress and anxiety on me, on my ex-husband, and on our family life. It affected our marriage at all levels.

Eventually, communication between us was an unfamiliar concept. Resentment was present. He was working long hours and under stress and I was trying to build a home and new life in a new environment, with no support from family, friends or him.

Marriage is a beautiful thing and should last forever but we tend to allow ourselves to get lost in the hundreds of things that distract us on a daily basis that are not as important as our marriage, and in turn, our personal and very important relationship loses value to us. We allow this to happen. We are to blame. But instead, we blame the job, coworkers, needy clients, long hours at work, lack of money, etc. because blaming others and things for our failures is easier than facing them and taking responsibility.

So if you ask me, I would say that Fairytales and perfect scenarios are a myth.

But 'happily ever after' is definitely possible. There are certain things you have to keep in mind and certain ways to keep a healthy relationship:

First, you need to listen to understand what the other is saying, not listen to respond, but listen to understand. There is a difference: When you listen only to respond, you miss the message, you are not listening to understand where your partner is coming from, how he/she really feels about a certain topic.

Trust is very important, to be sure of your feelings for one another. To trust is to have faith that you are with this person because you share a mutual love and respect for each other. When you trust and have faith there is no jealousy, and no drama.

Respect is key to keeping a healthy loving relationship alive. Respect yourself by not forgetting that you are your own person in this relationship, and you have a voice. Respect that your partner is his/her own person and he/she has a voice. It is not "WE" all the time. Do not loose yourself in the "WE."

Chemistry is important. Chemistry at all levels, physical, intellectual, and emotional. Let yourself go with the natural flow of how this beautiful relationship should evolve.

Keep up with the momentum as you did when you were first dating. Show your partner that you want to look your best for them, as that shows them that you care and want to keep that fire between you going strong.

The Dragonfly Effect / Samantha Cervino

I've learned we attract what we think about the most and we attract our partners either consciously or unconsciously. For a long time I thought my loving partners had come into my life by mere chance. I was unaware. I was wrong.

If I had known then what I know now I would have avoided so much heartache for myself. But, then again, each of my relationships taught me a lesson and made stronger and wiser as well. Now I definitely know what I do NOT want in a partner.

If you are single this is just what you need to do: Let me share an exercise that I learned from my mentor Bob Proctor, on how to attract your ideal mate into your life. Bob Proctor has a Youtube video on this titled **Attract a Specific Person Into Your Life**, and this is what you do: Draw a circle in the middle of a blanc sheet of paper. Inside this circle write the words "My man"/"My Woman."

From the circle draw lines in an outward direction like sun rays and on each line write down all the attributes you wish your man/woman to have. Be very specific!

Visualize this person in your mind, what he-she looks like, how he-she treats you, how you feel when you're with them. Imagine you've already found the person you're describing on this paper. But do not put a face to him/her. Let your imagination take you wherever it needs to go. Do not try to control it.

If you are consistent with this exercise I promise you that in time you will be attracted to this person. When you meet this person you will recognize the attributes he/she possesses, which are the same as those you consciously attracted into your energy field. You will share this unique chemistry and you will *know*.

The Dragonfly Effect / Samantha Cervino

It is very important to understand that all your relationships should be a positive influence in your life. Look for the company of those people who lift up your spirit, support you and help you in your journey to self-success.

I will share with you my thoughts about my marriage: I had almost everything I wished to have and yet I did not. Read on, and I will explain.

My husband and I had a vision for an abundant life. Our goals seemed to match, and in order to achieve those goals we moved a lot for his career and his success.

I made a conscious decision to support his career and because my intention was to stay at home and raise our son, I followed along and supported every decision my husband made but here is the tricky part and where I went wrong: I allowed him to make all the big decisions and I became totally dependant on him – and my voice as a wife and equal partner got quieter and quieter.

My son was my only focus and priority. My husband was so buried in work we barely communicated anymore. We had moved away from family and close friends, and because of this, I had no support. I didn't know how to express my unhappiness except by showing it.

My husband either ignored the signs or was simply oblivious that something was so wrong in our marriage. So we disconnected. He was always busy with work and had little time for me. The times I attempted to communicate it came across a nagging. It was frustrating!

I felt confused. Why was I unhappy when I was living the life I wanted? I moved four times for him, left everything behind to support him and keep our marriage together – and in the end, we lost our marriage.

The Dragonfly Effect / Samantha Cervino

The process I went through

I didn't have to work for a living. I had my perfect little boy. Yet, I felt this emptiness inside. I realized I was losing my husband and our communication was limited. When we spoke to each other it was not easy, as though we spoke two different languages. His career took over his life and I began to resent his job and him.

My husband disconnected and we lost what we once had. We failed to face the problems in our relationship and the only thing that did was made the problems worse and this created more distance between us. I would cry myself to sleep. My husband never knew, or noticed. Or perhaps he simply ignored my crying for fear of facing the real issue at hand. I will never know. All I know is that in my eyes he became a workaholic and avoided the problem that was staring him right in the face.

At times I thought that perhaps he was having an affair, but I could also see how much he had let himself go appearance-wise, so I was sure that was not it, he was not having an affair. I was sure he was not unfaithful to me. But we didn't have much of a life as loving partners either. It felt to me as though I was living with a roommate who happened to be the father of my child. And this is the way I lived for about five years until one day I said "enough!"

I had met someone who reminded me what it was like to feel chemistry and feel wanted. I did not participate fully in this episode in my life until I had decided to do so and had terminated my relationship with my husband. Nothing really happened there except I believe this person had come into my life to help me make a decision I was hesitating to make because leaving my husband would change my life forever in big ways, and I was terrified.

Sometimes people will show up in our life to show us a different way, to help us, to lift us up, and then they will just part ways and we never see them again.

After I asked my husband for a separation, he was devastated. I know I was hurting him but it was more painful to stay in the marriage than to start over. I tried to explain to him that this was the best solution for us as we lived in denial for years. I was really unhappy and so was he.

We separated but attempted to get back together after months apart. We took a trip to Los Cabos to see if we could start over but instead found ourselves on that New Year's Eve, sitting in our balcony in our suite overlooking the ocean, making the decision that a divorce was the way to go at this point. I felt no chemistry, nothing but a void in my being and just sadness. I had exhausted all my attempts to fix this chapter in my life.

Now, looking at all of this from both sides gives us a pretty good idea of where we fail in our personal relationships. Now we can re-examine our selves, our beliefs, our needs and our wants.

'Everlasting love' and 'happily-ever-after' do happen. But we may need to change our beliefs about them, our conditioning and habits by understanding first that we are the love that we seek.

We must understand and know that we are love. We do not need another person to love us in order for us to feel love. We are love. The idea of a relationship is to add joy and more love to our lives, to welcome someone to share our lives, dreams and desire to create a family and a new life.

There is no reason why two people can not get along and have a healthy relationship, but it takes a commitment from us to get to know the person we are with, their personality traits and how we can complement them and how they can complement us.

In a relationship it is not "my way or the highway" as it takes two to make it work, to take care of it, to nourish it. When we do not see eye-to-eye, instead of arguing or trying to force your partner to see things your way, try a different approach. Try Listening.

Lead by example, be creative, ask questions and try to understand why your partner is not agreeing with you. If it is something that can wait and your partner might be stressed about something then it may be wise to wait but of course let your partner know that you need to have this conversation with him/her as soon as possible. Show compassion and be there for your partner if you feel they are going through something. Offer your support and love.

When we are in an unhappy marriage or relationship we might blame our partner for our suffering. We may feel or believe that men/women lie to us, play us, use us and hurt us. But really, are they truly to blame? Or is it us, with all our high expectations that are setting the bar so high, that make people get confused and have a hard time just being themselves. What if we set the bar too high and do not accept them for who they really are?

This is a game we are playing and is not serving any of the players involved. I am not saying we are doing anything wrong. All I am saying is that from a very young age we are all misguided. Both men and women grow up with very different ideas about relationships and love.

Men tend to think differently, very simple and practical, for the most part. Women think more complexly, so much so that many times we cannot comprehend a man's mind.

It is important to have a conversation with our partner about what our intentions are for the relationship, what we want to create and co-create. Make sure you have all your questions answered before the big "I do," so there are no disappointments or surprises after the commitment is made and you can then have a nice flowing marriage and-or committed relationship with your loved one.

We often judge our partners for their past relationships and failures or they might judge us but why is it so important for us to judge? Is it to find out if they follow a pattern in choosing partners? Is it to test our own ego? Common questions often asked include: "How many partners have you had before me? How long was your last relationship? Were you previously married? Ask yourself why these questions matter when you meet a new potential mate.

In my professional and personal experience, I can tell you that people ask these questions out of personal insecurities. We are so insecure when we start a new relationship that we ask all these questions and find fault in our new partner and their past choices. We start to judge and then insecurities and jealousy start to show up. Many times your partner is not even aware this is happening in your head.

When you meet someone new, be open and accepting. Let it be easy and comfortable. You'll know as soon as you see this new person if he/she is someone you may want to see again. First dates are meant to be an ice-breaker not a pre-approval for a marriage application. Relax and be yourself.

"We all need that emotional support and encouragement from time to time so it is crucial that we allow ourselves to be vulnerable and allow people in our life. People who are a positive influence and can lift us up when we are down."
- Samantha Cervino

14: Tapping into Your Vulnerability

Vulnerability can be your greatest strength. It shows you have the courage to show up and be seen as you are.

Everyone is vulnerable and those who hide their vulnerability miss out on real intimacy in any relationship.

People tend to put up walls around them for fear of being hurt. But all this is part of life and you always learn from your experiences and the people you associate with.

You are human hence you have all these emotions to deal with but don't hide yourself from the world. Acknowledge the emotions but don't let them define you.

Vulnerability is less about the sender and more about the receiver. The receiver is the key here. To be vulnerable does not mean that you are weak.

For me, tapping into my vulnerability gives others permission to do the same. It builds a strong foundation of trust and transparency. As a healthcare provider, being in alignment with myself allows for more alignment in my life, thus what I am feeling, and experiencing is the same inside as outside. There is a safety that is tangible when one is vulnerable.

Further said, my desire is to lead by example. The bottom line is that we all want to be accepted and appreciated. In doing so, we allow and align to experience the abundance that the universe has to offer, which is already there for us. Being vulnerable is the first step to achieving this.

When we love someone we become emotionally vulnerable to those we love. If they are ill or suffering, we feel their pain and have a great deal of compassion. Children become vulnerable to their parents as their bonding grows.

You can benefit when you allow yourself to be vulnerable. As an example being connected to others is a basic human need and vulnerability gives you a sense of connectedness with humanity. Here are a couple of benefits:

A sense of belonging in a community: This ensures you have emotional support from others, forming new friendships and just having someone to talk to, laugh with and connect with on a deeper level.

Sharing your stories and trust in one another: Knowing you are not alone and feeling safe, increases your joy and lessens your pain. We live in a world that is very materialistic and independence is important.

Most individuals are consumed by work and planning for tomorrow so much so that the time to connect with others is minimal. With all the advances in technology, texting and email has become the norm. This takes away from that human connection we all need and which also allows us to express ourselves and be vulnerable.

We all need that emotional support and encouragement from time to time so it is crucial that we allow ourselves to be vulnerable and allow people in our life. People who are a positive influence and can lift us up when we are down. We have this power within ourselves already but we are humans and will have these life experiences when we will need a hand from a loved one and someone we trust and feel safe with.

It has been proven that a strong sense of belonging and close connection with others helps us recover quicker when we go through sad experiences or an illness. Showing how we really feel and allowing others to be there for us and support us gives us a chance to let go and accept with gratitude the people in our life and the joy they bring to us.

I find that people who are introverts find it more difficult to open up and share their thoughts and feelings as they are private and like to keep things to themselves.

The extrovert is talkative and outgoing, far more social in nature. So when it comes to being vulnerable the extrovert will be the one opening up and sharing.

Perhaps the extroverts find it easier to trust and confide in others, which opens the door to vulnerability in their life.

I think your level of confidence in yourself plays a big part in this because it allows for openness. Understanding your feelings and accepting your experience allows you to freely talk about it with others without fear of being judged.

It is when you do not have a clear understanding of your situation and life experience that you feel fear and doubt because not knowing what comes next for you can be frightening for some people. Vulnerability in this case is blocked by fear of being misunderstood, judged and ultimately hurt. This shows a lack of trust, confidence and faith in oneself and in God.

In personal relationships being vulnerable means that you are connecting with your partner. It is the driving force of connection. It is brave to be vulnerable. It is not weakness to show vulnerability, it shows your inner strength to express it.

People who suffer with addiction have the hardest time understanding that vulnerability is one way to set them free from the illness that is addiction.

Self-realization is an immense step to take for addicts and it goes hand in hand with being vulnerable. This is crucial for their recovery, to face their fears and 'blocks' that prevent them from moving forward into a healthy lifestyle.

Self-realization simply means taking a look at oneself, whom you truly are. No lies, no make up, no mask. It's all uncovered. It's just you looking at yourself, trying to understand who you are inside and out, with all your imperfections and negative habits.

You realize that you can change yourself and your life if you just acknowledge your blocks in life, which are the things and people that you perceive as being obstacles in your way. You can remove obstacles from your path once you make the decision to make changes and move some pieces around in your life.

Vulnerability involves healing your broken heart. This demands that you take a look at your whole life and be open to healing.

Most people tend to hide their pain and lock away all negative, painful events and throw away the key, never looking back. What this does to you is more damage in the long run. These emotions never heal and sit like cement in your solar plexus, where your stomach is located. This will cause you stress and stomach problems.

Emotions must be healed. It is not okay that you pretend all your hurts never happened. One must express these emotions and find a way to let it go. This is where vulnerability comes into play, it helps you heal and not hold anything back.

There are people that want to help you and love you. It is okay to show yourself. You are unique and a lovable being.

There are many that see vulnerability as a double-edged sword and I would like to talk about this a little further. Lets take a look at all the things that can happen to us when we open up. Being Vulnerable can put you at risk for injury, harm and heartbreak. Your defenses are down and your heart is open.

It also puts you at risk for rejection. Someone may reject you, dismiss you, judge you, or leave you. Being vulnerable puts you at risk for opening up old wounds. It means that someone may hurt you in the same way you've been hurt before. No one wants that!

Men in particular have a hard time with this and I wonder if this is ego based? Do men see vulnerability as a sign of weakness? I know of men that do feel that sharing and expressing their emotions is not a manly thing to do. They believe it is for women to be emotional and more attuned with feelings and talking about everything.

These men could not be more wrong. They have adapted this belief from generations. These are paradigms that must be redirected and eliminated because as I have explained in this chapter, vulnerability is power and in any healthy and long lasting relationship communication is key.

Showing up and being there for each other is crucial. Emotional support is a big requirement in any healthy relationship. So, if you are emotionally unavailable in your relationship, what do you think will happen to it?

But this is life and you are going to meet and come across all kinds of people and situations. Choose your company wisely by spending time with those whom make you feel good and are a positive influence in your life.

Learn from those who challenge you and embrace the experience because this helps you grow and understand more about humanity and yourself.

Do not let sad experiences and negative people affect you. Do not let them change you or make you feel that you cannot trust anyone.

You are a strong being with unlimited potential and being vulnerable has more benefits than not. Lets recap on all the positive and healing benefits of vulnerability.

Being vulnerable allows you to relate to others authentically. It means you don't have to pretend to be someone you are not. The people that truly love you are going to accept you for who you are, with all of your strengths and weaknesses.

Being vulnerable allows you to take risks and go after your dreams. It means you are able to live a life filled with passion, purpose, and joy.

It also allows you to experience true intimacy with others by connecting in a genuine, honest and loving way.

Being vulnerable allows you to give and receive real love.

And isn't real love what we all want?

15 - Healthy Relationships Guide

As we discussed, your relationships should be a positive influence in your life.

One way to really know if the people you most spend time with are a good influence on you is to write their names on a piece of paper and beside each of these people's names write down how you feel you about spending time with them. Do you feel excited or do you make excuses not to see them?

Your time is very valuable. How much time, energy and emotion do you give to people you don't wish to associate with and don't need in your life?

This can – and many times *does* – happen within families. Many times our family gives us grief, a bit of unwelcome drama and lack of support. And it is OK to give yourself some space away from them when you need it.

I had to pull away and put some distance with my own family.

At times I found myself feeling overwhelmed and suffocated involved in their drama. Automatically I was pulled into it and right in the middle of it. This caused major health issues in my life and much anxiety and stress.

Our time together was not joyful for me and I felt as though my energy was sucked right out of me, leaving me feeling frustrated and upset. It took a long time for me to understand that just because it's "family," doesn't mean I had to be involved in the drama or attend every single get-together.

Once, after I moved away to the USA for a few years with my then-husband and our little boy, I experienced peace for the first time and I realized that my being in a new location, was the medicine I needed.

I love each member of my family and I am not telling you or advising that you should not interact with your family if you can relate to what I went through… what I am saying is that it is okay to take time off to re charge and just be.

Check out your environmental conditioning… How do you feel in your close environment? If you hope to live a well-balanced life, answer this question. Most people are a product of their environment.

Now I see my family when it suits me, not them. I see them for the amount of time I want to see them, not the amount of time that might be expected, and I say no without feeling guilty. I learned to say "No" and my relationships with all of my family members are better now than ever before.

When it comes to romance though, here's a thought: Be specific about what you want, and what type of person you want to be with.

Always know and keep in mind that all people and relationships are different, and that you are different from the last person in your partner's life. Therefore you cannot and should not compare his or her ex partners with yourself and your unique relationship.

We all make mistakes and we all deserve a second chance. As long as communication is open and direct, you are sure to have success in your relationship.

Trust your intuition and check in with your heart. If it feels right then go with it.

If you see and feel that this man or woman is not what you wish for then politely say so and walk away. At the very least you might make a new friend.

When you come out of a relationship it is wise to give yourself some healing time.

Please understand that as you walk away from an unpleasant relationship you are in a low vibration from the disappointment and the law of attraction will bring another one to you that feels very much like the one you just walked out of and usually this happens quickly. This is why it is wise to wait and give yourself time to heal and get emotionally strong before you date again.

To attract the wanted relationship you wish to have you must reach for alignment between you and your inner self. This means that you have to take time to get yourself feeling good again as if you are not feeling good about yourself you will not be inspired to, nor be in the right vibration to attract into your life a positive loving relationship with another.

Feeling positive again can take months and sometimes years, finding yourself in an endless loop where you feel negative because of someone else, self-doomed blame.
Why is it anyone else's fault how you feel? Why are they in control of your emotions?

First, understand that an emotion is a feeling that will pass. Then understand that you have total control over your thoughts, feelings, emotions and actions.

Take responsibility for your life, as you, and only you are in control of your life. Nobody can "make" you feel a certain way or do something you do not want to do or take part in.

Taking responsibility for our own life is not an easy thing when you are accustomed to blaming others for the results in your life.

But once you take control and take responsibility, it is liberating: You experience freedom – and this is priceless.

If you take control over your own emotions you can think and improve positive thought because naturally it feels better to do so.

By turning the negative thought and turning it into a positive thought you will shift your vibration.

You see, you have no control over anyone else's actions or emotions but you do have complete control over your own thoughts, emotions and vibrations and point of attraction!

Conclusion:

There is light at the end of the tunnel and God is with you, within you. God is your strength, it's the love you feel and the love that you are.

My first lesson I learned was that I was the love I was seeking from others. I was complete on my own. Every time I felt defeated, I got up again and kept going forward as that was my inner strength that is God within me. Every time I looked up at the sky and looked to God for answers, following my undying faith, it was God trying to show me that light, the light that I am.

When I finally had enough with my life the way it had been for years, I made a decision to change things *for me*. I would look at myself in the mirror and see pain in my eyes, always hiding behind an empty smile. I felt deep inside that I was more than what I was seeing reflected in the mirror. I knew I was denying myself freedom, happiness and love.

This was spirit telling me to get out of my own way and start loving myself and respecting myself. What a new concept that was for me, to respect myself and to love me, to accept me with all my beautiful imperfections.

I wasn't weak, but I was scared. I chose freedom, love and happiness knowing God had a better plan for me and that I was love and loved.

My first lesson was the most important one of all: To start a relationship with me, I had to like me, love me, respect me, accept me and forgive me. And all this I had to do on my own, to find my true self. To like me was easy, to love me took a little more time and deeper understanding of how it was that I didn't love me already. Energy healing helped me so much with self-love and self-acceptance.

Accepting my whole life with all the experiences good and bad and all the people in my life past and present. Trying to understand my habitual patterns and the part that I played in all situations. Accepting, releasing and forgiving.

Releasing the bad and challenging situations and people to God and the universe allowed me to move forward and let go of resentment and painful memories. Learn from those experiences from your past and turn the page as if it were chapters in a book.

The forgiveness was tough because I had to relive the experience and forgive it, forgive those who had hurt me and forgive myself for feeling hate and resentment for so long. I finally understood that a feeling of anger, hate and frustration was hurting me most of all. When we hurt our heart this way, with these negative feelings, we are putting ourselves in a very low energetic vibration and this affects our life in all aspects including our health.

I wish I knew then what I know now. I am sure you say that sometimes too. But it takes time to learn a life lesson and some of us are here to learn certain things that we need to master before we can move on to the next phase of our life and existence in this world.

Positive thinking is essential for a healthy body and mind. Though deep inside I was always a positive person and that is what always encouraged me to continue: A positive mind and my undying faith. I did not know nor was I aware of the fact that I could control my thoughts.

A thought is an idea, an opinion produced by thinking. It creates a feeling, which affects your vibration. Every thought creates into a form and your physical experience is a reflection of your thoughts. This is why it is vital for your well being to keep a positive mind and let this positiveness be the rule and driving force of your mind.

You become what you think about the most and thoughts are things. The body will do what the mind tells it to do.

Positive thoughts equal positive results.

Your conscious mind has the ability to accept and reject any thought or idea you give to it. So why not only accept the positive and productive thoughts? This affects the vibration you are in.

Your subconscious mind does not have the ability to reject and so it only accepts what the conscious mind and your belief sends to it. Your subconscious mind feels and becomes the vibration your are in thus sends out waves of either poor low vibration or high positive vibrations. This is what you are seeding out to the universe and whatever vibration you are in is what you attract.

By keeping your mind positive and redirecting any low vibration thoughts and shifting it into a positive thought, takes constant practice and consistency but it is the way to convince your subconscious mind and start to change your energetic vibration.

Autosuggestion and affirmations are a key component in achieving this ultimate consistent positive mind and attitude. Autosuggestion is self-talk we give ourselves. Make it loving and positive. Say only the best about yourself no matter how bad you may feel at the moment.

Fight that feeling off with autosuggestion and affirmations!

Here are some examples you can say: "I am so happy and grateful for my positive and creative mind." "I am a beautiful person, proactive and successful." "My life is abundant. I only attract loving and positive experiences into my life."

Gratitude is essential and the best way to start your day. It helps fight off negative feelings and shifts thoughts from negative to positive. It changes your attitude so you feel happy and enthusiastic. By expressing gratitude for the things and people that are present in your life adding more joy and love to your life, you put yourself in harmony with the things you desire. Believe that you can have all that you want.

The universe is abundant and there is plenty for all. Be sure to follow these steps, ask for what you want and nothing less. Prepare yourself to receive it. Stay focused on your goals. Stay positive and make good use of your time. Have a good attitude toward life and life will have a good attitude toward you.

Attitude is the refection of you. How you are really feeling inside, shows on the outside. This indicates your feelings, your actions and your thoughts. You are in control of your attitude. Have a positive loving attitude and be in a good vibration to change your life, your circumstance and feel successful. Attract what you want! Attitude is the most important action you can take, the first step into a happier more abundant life. Good attitude, good results.

Make good use of your time. Are your busy doing things? Or are you busy getting things done? There's a big difference here, so ask yourself this question and be honest when you answer.

Challenge yourself and write down all the things you do in one day, hour by hour. This will give you a pretty good idea of whether you are making good use of your time or not. Are you being proactive? Do you get yourself involved in conversation that has no real meaning? Do you spend hours in front of the TV? Do you feel bored more times than not thinking there is nothing to do?

If you really want to change your results you have to make changes and make decisions. I would like for you, starting now, to make a list of six things that you can do tomorrow that will help you achieve your goal and make your day a productive one. Do this every night. Even if you don't get all the things on your list done tomorrow leave the rest for the next day and so on but make sure you do not get distracted with the meaningless. This will really help if you keep focused! Your time is valuable so don't waste it!

People with goals always succeed because they know where they are going. They keep focused on the goal and do not allow external negativity to distract them. Successful people read, study, and mastermind. They make really good use of their time. Surround yourself with those whom you can learn from and those that will support your dreams and ambitions. It is okay to want more and aspire for more. This is a sign that you are evolving and wanting to live abundantly.

Of course, do not lose focus on the really important things in your life as you follow your dream or goal. Do not lose the love in your life and do not hurt anyone in the process of you achieving your success. Do not let success get to your head.

Be smart and don't be scared to take risks. Do not let fear stop you, it always happens that when we are about to reach a breakthrough we hit the terror barrier and we may stop and get really scared and maybe take a step back out of fear of the unknown.

Let me assure you that when you get to that point it is best to walk right through that terror barrier because what is behind it, waiting for you, is your success. Your fears disappear the moment you stop paying attention to them.

The important fact here is that it is not so much about achieving goals. What matters most is how you grow in the process: Your inner growth, your evolution, you allowing yourself to try new things and be fierce about your dreams.

It is about you creating, learning and growing, expanding your horizons and testing your limitless potential. Using your intellectual faculties the best way possible.

Your will, imagination, intuition, perception, memory and reason are all powers of the mind that you are gifted with. You did not have to go and acquire them they were always in you. Use them well.

The imagination is a wonderful tool. When you were a young child you used to daydream all the time and imagine a perfect life for yourself.

But one day at school and at home some adults most likely asked you to stop dreaming and pay attention. Well, dreaming is great and you should dream up the life of your dreams because you deserve to live it! But dreaming alone won't get you there. Here is how all your mental faculties put together help you manifest your desires.

Your will gives you the ability to focus on your idea and that push you need to make it happen.

Your will is when you give yourself a command and follow through with it. Like with self-discipline you need your will to be disciplined. It is your ability to concentrate and your inner strength to keep going.

Intuition is God talking to you. This is the voice of spirit guiding you in the right path. When you ask a question, listen to that voice of reason, which unfortunately many times we ignore because we'd rather listen to our intellect.

Intuition is not a sixth sense it is a mental factor and it comes as a sudden idea or answer to a question.

I always say listen with your heart, if it feels right it *is* right and if you are not sure don't do it, better to wait. But the voice of intuition will always be the first one you hear.

Your perception is your point of view. How you see things. There is no right or wrong here because we all see things differently.

You might be looking at an object with another person and each of you will see something unique about it that is not what the other person may see. It's the same with a situation: You may think a particular situation is good and the other person may think it is not.

We perceive things differently. Your perception determines your attitude and yes, you can change your point of view or your perception about anything by changing your attitude about it.

Your memory is perfect. We have unlimited ability to memorize and learn anything we want and as much as we want. But we need to want this. We need to exercise our memory and feed it with knowledge, study, memory games, books, word cross puzzles etc.

There is no such thing as a 'bad memory' and people that say this just haven't learned how to develop this mental muscle at a higher level.

Reason is what gives us the ability to think. Mental activity does not constitute thinking!

To think is to be consciously aware of the thoughts and ideas that come to our mind, and to choose to reject or accept them into our reality.

So knowing how to use these mental faculties that you were born with, in a way that they serve you for you to achieve your goals and live a well-balanced life is essential for your wonderful future.

Reading books on self-development such as this one, or others such as **The Power of your Subconscious Mind** by Joseph Murphy or **Think and Grow Rich** by Napoleon Hill, will help you.

These books have taught me everything I know but also you must apply these concepts and knowledge into your daily life, in everything you do and how your think from now on. It is the only way you will change your circumstances.

Changing your thoughts and your attitude are the first steps you must take.

What does it mean to live a well-balanced life? It means to live a life in which you are in peace with yourself.
You have money-freedom, time-freedom, you are in harmony with the universal laws.

Your power within is poise and peace. You have let go of anything that no longer serves you.

In the book **The Game of Life and How to Play it** by Florence Scovel Shinn, she reminds us that the game of life is like a boomerang: Whatever you send out ultimately comes back to you.

Also, you attract what your fear the most just as easily as you can attract what you want the most. It is all in your thoughts! This is so crucial to comprehend that your thoughts are things and you become what you think about.

Your ruling thoughts in your mind should be positive, loving, empathetic and productive. Gratitude will serve you well.

Gratitude is the law of increase and complaint is the opposite. Complaint is the law of decrease.

Here is an affirmation from my book The Gratitude Affirmations that you should say out loud every day:

"I am so happy and grateful now that I am in control of my thoughts. I only allow positive thoughts to enter my mind. My thoughts are creative, loving and productive!"

Say it with conviction!

The key that unlocks energy is 'Desire'. It's also the key to a long and interesting life.

"If we expect to create any drive, any real force within ourselves, we have to get excited."
- Earl Nightingale

A Final Note

Sharing my story with you in this book has been an absolute honour. My intention and hope is that what I shared with you serves you well and inspires you to self-develop yourself and grow in faith and wisdom. Everything is here for you: All you have to do is say 'yes' to change, and opportunity for inner growth. Make a commitment to yourself that you will make the time to expand your horizons.

I encourage you to refer to the material and books I have recommended including my own.

Trust in yourself, trust in God, the universe. Relax and be present. Practice gratitude everyday. Take control over your dominating thoughts to shift from negative to positive. Read this book over and over again, specially the chapters that resonate most with you.

Every time you read it you will see something you didn't notice before, you will grow in awareness each time. Put all you have learned here into action remember that knowledge alone will not give you the results you desire. Time, commitment, persistence, faith, continues study or reading, self-growth and a positive mind these are all the ingredients you need.

"Whatever we plant in our subconscious mind and nourish with repetition and emotion will one day become reality"
- Earl Nightingale

About the Author

For many years Samantha Cervino worked with children diagnosed with ADD, ADHD, Asperger, Dyslexia and Autism. She has changed and improved the lives of many children, as well as countless clients in her practice of energy healing and self-development coaching. She is committed to helping guide her clients and humanity toward achieving a well-balanced life.

In addition to being an accomplished leader in her field of understanding and shifting human emotions through Reiki, EFT Tapping and continuous studies in self development, the human mind, achieving personal success and the universal laws, Samantha, with her experience and vast knowledge, is able to help others learn what it takes to meet their goal and show them how to tap into their endless potential.

She is also a blogger, published author, and Wellness Universe Ambassador, who motivates through her work on social media by sharing great insights by the world's greatest minds and teaching her audience about the importance of gratitude and affirmations.

Samantha believes in giving back to humanity. For many years she has sponsored a child in Africa. She also gives of her time to serve in her community as a peer counsellor at the Women's Centre. As well, she facilitates support groups for changing results.

As a master energy healer, Samantha is committed to the personal success of her clients and is often quoted for her stated belief: "Life is to be felt, not planned."

For more information visit: www.smbalternativehealing.me or email Samantha Cervino at: samcp10@gmail.com

The Dragonfly Effect / Samantha Cervino

Manor House
905-648-2193
www.manor-house-publishing.com

www.ingramcontent.com/pod-product-compliance
Lightning Source LLC
Chambersburg PA
CBHW070108080526
44586CB00013B/1224